BLACK BRITISH HISTORY
Black Influences on British Culture (1948 to 2016)
32 Hours of Teaching and Learning Material for Parents, Guardians, and Teachers of Secondary School Students

D1438213

BLACK BRITISH HISTORY
Black Influences on British Culture (1948 to 2016)
32 Hours of Teaching and Learning Material for Parents, Guardians, and Teachers of Secondary School Students

BY

Robin Walker, Vanika Marshall, Paula Perry and Anthony Vaughan

With a Foreword by Tony Warner

REKLAW EDUCATION LIMITED &
CROYDON SUPPLEMENTARY EDUCATION PROJECT
London (U.K.)

BLACK BRITISH HISTORY: Black Influences on British Culture (1948 to 2016)
Published in 2017

ISBN-13: 978-1975619732

ISBN-10: 1975619730

CONTENTS

The paradox of education is precisely this – that as one begins to become conscious one begins to examine the society in which he is being educated.
James Baldwin, 1963

If you struggled to identify any of the 33 people on the covers of this book, **Black British History: Black Influences on British Culture (1948 to 2016),** ask yourself why.

Black British history has been actively suppressed for a very long time. This suppression has led to alarming ignorance and low self-esteem. How does one explain that children in Britain are religiously taught every detail on Rosa Parks and the Montgomery Alabama Bus Boycott of 1955, but are *not* taught anything about the bus boycott in Bristol, England, which took place in 1963?

Most adults cannot name or even *recognise* the leader of this Black British civil rights campaign. His photo is on the back of this book, and his activities laid the groundwork for the *Race Relations Acts of 1963, 1965, 1976, 2000* as well as the *Equality Act* of *2010*. Surely, this history is both Black and British and worthy of inclusion in any secondary school teaching resource.

While the average adult will know what 'bussing' means when applied to American history, why are they totally unaware that in Haringey, Ealing, and other parts of England, Black and Asian children were bussed out of areas where it was felt there were 'too many of them', and their presence would bring down the achievement of White children?

Parents, teachers, and students have consistently complained about the lack of diversity in the National Curriculum and the accompanying dearth of resources. Even when incremental improvements were made, there have been efforts to reverse them: in 2012, when Michael Gove was Secretary for Education, he tried to reduce the already scarce Black presence in the Curriculum by removing the figures of Mary Seacole and Olaudah Equiano. Forty thousand petitioners objected and over 100 MPs and celebrities said 'no', so those outstanding historical greats remain – but there should be more.

The cost of not acknowledging the historical contributions of Black people in the British educational system is high. Most recently, we have seen how this has led to a level of ignorance in the national consciousness resulting in White female historian and presenter, Mary Beard, being viciously trolled for daring to state that there were, in fact, Blacks in Roman Britain.

Endless studies have been produced which explicitly state that what and how people are taught can affect their personality. In 1971, Bernard Coard pointed out how the Black child's self-esteem was negatively impacted by the British education system in his legendary booklet *How the West Indian Child is Made Educationally Subnormal in the British School System*. Going further back, in the 1954 'Doll Test' which questioned children about black and white dolls, it was found that both Black and White children expressed negative anti-black attitudes about the black doll. The creator of the test, Dr Kenneth Clarke, complained that his evidence in the case of Brown versus Board of Education was only partially quoted by the court; specifically, his finding was that racism "twisted the personality of white as well as black children".

This book with its broad sweep from 1948 to 2016 is perfect to address the imbalances already referred to. The harried teacher trying to find history to reflect their classroom; the home-schooler looking for authentic content, and the general reader who just wants to broaden their knowledge of a history that includes Black people will find this text a relief, a support, and a solid building block, to a fairer society.

As relevant in rural areas like Dorset or Norfolk as it is in Inner London, this book is for teachers who might like to educate their class in something other than the annual stale repeats of American Black history.

This is an engaging, well-researched and comprehensive text that you can buy on Friday and put to work on Monday. It will certainly help to address the paradox of education, which presently sees Black and White British children misinformed and rendered 'unconscious' of their own country's history.

Tony Warner
info@blackhistorywalks.co.uk

HOW TO USE THIS BOOK

Black British History: Black Influences on British Culture (1948 to 2016) is aimed at parents and teachers who would like solid information to teach their children Modern Black British History, and to exercise the historical skills required by the National Curriculum. The book does NOT deal with earlier chapters of Black British history. We intend to fill this gap with subsequent publications.

The material is designed for children at Key Stage 3 Level – i.e. young people aged 11 to 14. The lessons can work with slightly older or younger people. We, for example, have profitably used this material with adults.

The first lesson begins in 2011 and discusses Black British influence on the Chav subculture. The second lesson goes back to beginnings with the SS Empire Windrush in 1948. The other 30 classes follow chronologically from 1948 to 2016 dealing with politics and culture, and the role Black British people played. The book also contains a *Picture Appendix,* a discussion of Black History in the English National Curriculum, and short biographical sketches of the writers.

This book highlights Black Migrant, African American and Black British influences on the host community. However, it must be noted that cultural influences are always multi directional. Black Migrant culture has massively been shaped by being in the UK. Thus, Black Migrant culture evolved into Black British culture by adopting influences from the host Anglo-Saxon-Jutish and Celtic cultures. Moreover, the book narrates how Black Britain gradually won acceptance as a part of British mainstream culture through the avenues of boxing, athletics, football, art, textiles, literature, drama, and politics.

To our knowledge, no book aimed at schoolchildren carries this empowering content.

Parents should be aware that each lesson lasts about one hour in length and may be structured like this.
(1) The students should WRITE the Class Title and the Learning Objective into their notebook or on a sheet of paper. This should take about one minute.
(2) The parent or teacher should lead the students in READING and DISCUSSING the material and the sources. The students should STUDY the relevant illustrations from the *Picture Appendix* as well. One effective strategy is to instruct the students to take turns in reading a sentence or paragraph aloud each, one after the other. The reading and the discussion should take about fifteen to twenty minutes in total.
(3) The students should give WRITTEN answers to the Activity questions in their notebook or on the sheet of paper. This should take most of the remaining forty or so minutes. They do not need to copy out the questions unless the activity specifically asks them to, but they must write answers in full sentences.
(4) The parent or teacher should CHECK over the answers with the students in the last five minutes.
(5) If any students finish early, get them to sketch something relevant from the *Picture Appendix* into their notebooks.

School Teachers who are reading this will, of course, be able to come up with far more inventive ways to work through these lessons.

CLASS ONE: CHALLENGING AN IGNORANT HISTORIAN

Learning Objective: To learn how history can be used to challenge modern preconceptions

On 12 August 2011, Dr David Starkey, a British historian, appeared on *Newsnight* and said something shocking. He compared Black British culture to Jamaican gangsterism. He said:

[A] substantial section of the Chavs ... have become Black. The Whites have become Black; a particular sort of violent, destructive, nihilistic, gangster culture has become the fashion and Black and White, boy and girl operate in this language together. This language, which is wholly false, which is this Jamaican Patois that's been intruded in England and this is why so many of us have this sense of literally a foreign country.

The Chavs were a White working class urban subculture that became dominant in the 2000s. Their style icons were Katie Price and Daniella Westbrook. Influenced by African American HipHop and R & B, also Black British Garage and Grime, the Chavs wore designer label sportswear, baseball caps, gold chains, sovereign rings, and large hoop earrings. Some of their speech patterns show traces of 'Jafaican' a multicultural version of English. The key non-Black influence in Chav style was the wearing of Burberry check patterns.

Dr David Starkey suggested that Black influence on Chav culture has produced something unique: The Whites have become Black. However, in this book we will show that there is nothing new or unique about this. It has happened several times before. The main problem is that few people have documented Black influences on White working-class culture. This is how it is possible for Dr Starkey, a professional historian, to embarrass himself on national television. He revealed to the world just how little he knows about British history.

Moreover, other Whites share this condescending and negative attitude towards the Chavs. Catherine Tate, a British comedian, created a Chav comedy character called Lauren Cooper who had the catchphrase: "Am I bovvered!" Matt Lucas, another comedian, created another Chav character, Vicky Pollard.

In this book, we will show that Black people in Britain influenced several White working-class subcultures: the Mods, the Skinheads, the Punks, the 2 Tone movement, and the Chavs. Moreover, African American culture influenced the Teddy Boys. It also impacted on the Mods and the Chavs. None of this is new. Cultures always influence each other. Even the Rave and Acid House subcultures are of African American origin.

Finally, we will show how Black Britain gradually won acceptance as a part of British mainstream culture through the avenues of boxing, athletics, football, art, textiles, literature, drama, and politics.

Source A
What does the word 'chav' mean? ... It's a word that's used to ridicule and label people who come from a less educated background than the rest of society. For me, it's no different from similar words used to denigrate people's race or sex ... If you did the same thing with race or sex, there'd be public uproar, and rightly so.
(Rapper Plan B, interviewed in *Plan B: don't call me a chav,* in *Radio Times,* 17 June 2012)

'Chav' is quite a clever word because it has a comic component. There's something quite funny about Chavs: their bad taste, their haircuts, their lifestyles seems almost comically grotesquely vulgar.
(Toby Young, interviewed in *The History of Now: The Story of the Noughties*, BBC television, 2010)

They were full of themselves, they were quite into bling, they were White, and they were tattooed. What they now call ... the 'tramp stamp' which is at the small of the back, on the 'muffin top'. A 'tramp stamp' on the 'muffin top' on a Chav. That tells you a lot about English as it has developed in the last ten years.
(Andrew Marr, interviewed in *The History of Now: The Story of the Noughties*, BBC television, 2010)

If you struggle to understand Cockney, Brummie, Geordie and Scouse, then stand by for an even bigger challenge. It's called Jafaican and, slowly but surely, it is infiltrating the English language. The multicultural hybrid, based on Jamaican but with undertones of West African and Indian, is ... becoming so common in the inner cities that it is beginning to eclipse traditional accents.
(Laura Clark, *'Jafaican' is wiping out inner-city English accents*, in *Daily Mail*, 12 April 2006)

ACTIVITIES . . .

1. Who was Dr David Starkey and why is he important?

2. Which elements of Chav subculture did African American or Black British culture directly influence? What elements seem to be uninfluenced by Black culture?

3. Using Source D and other data, what is 'Jafaican'?

4. What is the factual error in Dr Starkey claiming that 'The Whites have become Black'? Why is this an embarrassing thing for a British historian to say?

5. According to Source A, why should it be unacceptable to speak negatively about Chavs?

6. Copy and complete this table.

Source	Information about Chavs	Impression about Chavs
David Starkey (Paragraph 2)		
Toby Young (Source B)		
Andrew Marr (Source C)		

7. In your opinion, why do you think that David Starkey, Toby Young and Andrew Marr are so negative about the Chavs?

CLASS TWO: SS EMPIRE WINDRUSH AND THE BEGINNINGS OF MODERN BLACK BRITAIN

Learning Objective: How did Modern Black Britain begin?

Modern Black Britain began in 1948. Nearly five hundred Caribbean people, mostly men, arrived at Tilbury Docks in Essex. This is not too far from London. They arrived from Jamaica on a ship called the SS Empire Windrush. Most of the voyagers were Jamaicans but one hundred came from other Caribbean countries and Guyana. Britain ruled these countries as part of the British Empire.

There were, of course, Black people living in Cardiff and Liverpool who were descended from much earlier movements of people. The single most famous person of Pre Windrush heritage is the musician Dame Shirley Bassey. She is of Welsh and Nigerian heritage.

At the time, Caribbean people saw England as the 'Mother Country' of the British Empire. A lot of the young men were former soldiers who fought in World War II. Most were smartly dressed in sharp suits, ties, colourful trilby hats and fashionable shoes. They arrived with a mood of hope and excitement, to start a new life in the 'Mother Country'. Many other Caribbeans, South Americans and West Africans would also sail to Britain.

Despite the SS Empire Windrush leaving from Jamaica, the people on the ship of cultural importance were the Trinidadians such as Lord Kitchener, Lord Beginner, and Lord Woodbine. On arrival at Tilbury Docks, Lord Kitchener sang live for the main news outlet Pathé News. He wrote his experiences into his music, using the dominant Calypso style from Trinidad. To land on the soil of the 'Mother Country', seemed like an adventure.

Lord Woodbine was also a famous Calypsonian. His group, 'Lord Woodbine and his Trinidadians', were amongst the first to go on tour in England. Kitchener and Woodbine introduced Calypso to Britain.

The Caribbean arrivals were housed in buildings that were originally World War II Air Raid Shelters under Clapham Common. They came to England to plug a labour shortage caused by World War II. As soon as they found work, they had to leave the Air Raid shelter. Most settled near to where they could find work. For most, this was in London. For others, this was in Manchester and the West Midlands.

Source A
Five Hundred Pairs of Willing Hands.
(This was the headline for a 1948 newspaper article by Peter Fryer)

Source B
London is the place for me,
London this lovely city,
You can go to France or America,
India, Asia or Australia,
but you must come back to London City
(Lord Kitchener sung this on his arrival at Tilbury Docks, *Pathé Reporter Meets,* British Pathé news, June 1948)

I am a single man only my mother that is depending on me and I am also an ex-Service man ... RAF. I took a course in Scotland in case making ... I am trying to help myself and also help my mom.
(Passenger on board SS Empire Windrush said this on his arrival, *Pathé Reporter Meets,* British Pathé news, June 1948)

Source D
It must be noted that there were Africans in Britain from Roman Times.
(Tony Sewell, *Keep On Moving: The Windrush Legacy,* p. 1)

ACTIVITIES . . .

1. Copy this out and fill in the gaps

Modern Black Britain began in _____ . _____ Caribbean people arrived at _____ _____ in Essex. At the time, Caribbean people saw England as the _____ _____ of the _____ _____. The _____ arrivals were housed near _____ _____ . They came to England to help a _____ _____ caused by World War II.

| 500 | British Empire | Clapham Common | 1948 |
| labour shortage | Tilbury Docks | Mother Country | Caribbean |

2. Why were the Trinidadians on the ship of cultural importance?

3. What was important about Clapham Common?

4. According to Source A, why were the Caribbeans of importance to Britain? What state was England in after World War II?

5. According to Source B and the other information about the 'Mother Country', how did Caribbeans see England at that time?

6. Using Source C, give one more reason Caribbeans came to Britain.

7. With reference to Source D, why do historians use the term 'Modern' Black Britain to refer to 1948 onwards?

EXTENDED WRITING

From your imagination, write a *Dear Diary* from the perspective of a Caribbean man on board the SS Empire Windrush. Write about your hopes, ambitions, and fears about coming to England.

Learning Objective: What was the first musical culture Black Migrants brought to the UK?

Calypso is a style of African-Caribbean music. It originated in Trinidad and Tobago in the early 20th century. From there it spread to the rest of the Caribbean. The musical elements of Calypso can be traced back to Africa. Africa has a similar form of music called Highlife. Calypso musicians played trumpets, trombones, saxophones, double basses, congas, bongos, steelpans, violins, maracas, and bamboo sticks.

The SS Empire Windrush brought nearly 500 passengers from the Caribbean. The Trinidadians aboard the ship brought Calypso to Britain. Calypso gained popularity amongst Britons of all origins. Calypso helped Caribbean music gain international recognition.

Lord Kitchener was already a star in Trinidad. In London, he performed for Caribbean and West African audiences. However, he also became popular with music hall and variety show audiences. He sang for Princess Margaret. Kitchener's song *London is the Place for Me* described the experience of the Windrush generation. Some of his songs, like *White and Black* and *Africa My Home,* spoke against the racism he met in Britain. He wrote a song dedicated to Ghana when this country became the first African country to become independent of British rule in 1957. Other songs were more playful.

Edric Connor, a Trinidadian actor and singer, starred in a West End musical called *Calypso.* This 1948 show was the first London play based on a West Indian subject with a Caribbean cast (see page 65). He also recorded *Songs from Trinidad* and *Songs from Jamaica* in 1954 and 1955. These were the first recordings of Caribbean Folk Music in the United Kingdom.

The 1951 *Festival of Britain* brought the Trinidad All Steel Percussion Orchestra to the attention of the British public. They created a trend for wealthy and stylish English people in Oxford and Cambridge to hire Steel bands and other Calypso musicians for debutante parties.

Winifred Atwell was a Trinidadian pianist. A brilliant music student, she studied at London's Royal Academy of Music. Specialising in the African American musical styles of Ragtime and Boogie Woogie rather than Calypso, Atwell reached number 1 in the album charts several times in the 1950s. She was the star of three television series on British television in 1954 and 1955. She is still the only female instrumentalist in British history to reach number 1. Her popularity in Britain included playing at a private party for Queen Elizabeth II, and was called back for an encore by the Queen herself!

In 1959 Claudia Jones, the great civil rights fighter, assisted by Edric Connor, started the St Pancras Carnival. Based on Trinidadian Calypso themed carnivals, the St Pancras Carnival evolved into Notting Hill Carnival.

Finally, in 1962, Lord Kitchener chose to return to the Caribbean. Black Britain had lost its most important cultural voice.

Source A

[Af]ter the second world war, a succession of black music's have transformed the British music scene. Ska, bluebeat and, of course, reggae were followed by rap, dance-hall, "jungle", techno and house. But the oldest of these musical forms is the calypso--the music and lyrics associated with the Trinidad Carnival--which, according to Lloyd Bradley, became "the official sound-track of black Britain" in the 1950s and early 1960s.
(Stuart Hall, *Calypso Kings: Notting Hill Carnival 2002,* in *The Guardian,* 28 June 2002)

Source B

Calypso originated in Trinidad as a means of public comment. Writing about its sometimes sexually explicit content, Jonathan Skinner argues that 'as both the medium and mode of social expression, of social institutions, social issues, ills and opinions calypso is explicitly a form of social commentary, and calypso as social commentary can be very explicit in its content'.
(Jon Stratton, *When Music Migrates: Crossing British and European Racial Faultlines, 1945-1910,* 2014)

Source C

Mama Rhythm is Africa. Africa's children in the Western Hemisphere used different means of expressing their closeness to Mama. The Brazilian Africans created the samba, the West Indians created the calypso, the Cubans created the rhumba and various other rhythms, and my own [i.e. African Americans] is blues, spirituals.
(Dizzy Gillespie, *To Be or not To Bop,* p. 483)

Source D

Sterling Betancourt, a performer in the Trinidad All Steel Percussion Orchestra, recalled the impact of his 1951 performance in London.
Well that day it was very funny because we purposely did not paint the drums. They leave it all rusty and well, looking like dustbin ... People start to laugh ... They giggling: 'What these Black men going to do with these old dustbins?' When we start up everybody was shocked. They were looking to see where the music coming from and said: 'Wow, this is Black Magic!'
(*TASPO | Sterling Betancourt | The 1951 Festival of Britain,* YouTube, 29 September 2011)

ACTIVITIES . . .

1. What was Calypso? How did Calypso become popular in Britain?

2. What was the significance of Lord Kitchener?

3. Write 5 facts about Winifred Atwell.

4. Produce a timeline of the most important facts about The Calypso Years from 1948 to 1962.

5. According to Source A, how did Black people change the music of Britain?

6. According to Source B, for what reasons might some people have objected to Calypso?

7. According to Source C, in what way is Calypso connected to Samba, Rhumba, Blues, and Spirituals?

8. Source D uses English words, but the grammar of the phrases is very different. Why do you think this is?

Learning Objective: How the Teddy Boys adopted Rock and Roll but hated Black Migrants

The Caribbean arrivals encountered prejudice when they attempted to find homes and work. It was a culture shock for many English people. Some had not seen a Black person let alone having one living next door to them. Another challenge came from the Teddy Boys, a tough working-class White subculture. The Teddy Boys gained a frightening reputation for gang activity, flick knives and anti-Black violence.

Strangely enough, Rock and Roll culture heavily influenced the Teddy Boys. Rock and Roll, however, originally came from Black America. What complicated this story was the fact that it was White American imitators of Rock and Roll like Bill Haley and Elvis Presley who were the first Americans to become popular in Britain. Consequently, many Teddy Boys may have been unaware of the Black origins of Rock and Roll.

Rock and Roll was a type of music that started in the United States. It developed from musical styles such as Gospel, Rhythm & Blues, and Boogie Woogie in the early 1950s. African Americans Fats Domino, Little Richard and Ike Turner started this new music. Chuck Berry, another African American, fused Rock and Roll with White Hillbilly music to create Rockabilly. Though they have undergone many changes, Rock & Roll and Rockabilly are still the popular musical forms of today.

Rock and Roll influenced fashion, attitudes, and language. Both Black Americans and White American teens enjoyed the music. It began to shape the American youth and created the first teenage culture. Prior to this period, people either lived the lifestyles of adults or children. There was nothing in between.

White British artists such as Tommy Steele, also Cliff Richard & the Shadows, attempted to copy this style of music in around the mid 1950s. It replaced an earlier form of Pop and Folk music in Britain called Skiffle. However, the first known appearance of Rock and Roll on BBC television was a performance by the Southlanders in 1955. They were a Jamaican vocal group based in South London. The first group of British youngsters to turn Rock & Roll and Rockabilly into a subculture were the Teddy Boys.

Despite deriving a subculture from American music of Black origins, the Teddy Boys were racists and encouraged violence against Black people. The most well-known incidents were in 1958. The Teddy Boy attacks culminated in the Notting Hill anti-Black race riots.

Source A
[T]hey had ... adopted ... long jackets ... tight 'drainpipe' trousers ... a string tie ... tied in a bow, and shoes which came to a point called 'winklepickers,' or shoes with thick synthetic soles ... called 'brothel creepers' ... topped off with a well greased mop of hair, with a lock falling over the forehead.
(Mike Phillips & Trevor Phillips, *Windrush*, 1998, p. 161)

Source B
The Teddy Boys is a uniquely British phenomenon and pre-dates the introduction of American Rock'n'Roll music into Britain in late 1955 by Bill Haley & his Comets by at least five years or so. However, one fact is clear, that when Rock'n'Roll did hit Britain like a thunderbolt in 1955, the music

would quickly become adopted by Britain's Teddy Boys and from that point onwards the style and the music became inseparable.
(John Van Rheede Toas aka Rockin Nidge, *History of the British Teddy Boy Movement,* from *The Edwardian Teddy Boy* website)

Source C
We put a record on ... I went 'what's going on here?' Little Richard man. Rock and Roll and it just hit Skiffle a knockout blow ... to the jaw. And that was the end of Skiffle.
(Musician Joe Brown explains how Rock and Roll replaced England's earlier Pop and Folk music, Skiffle in *50s Britannia: Rock and Roll Britannia,* BBC television, 2013)

Source D
Under its influence youths and girls jive in the gangways of cinemas and tear up the seats ... It is deplorable, it is tribal and it is from America. It follows Ragtime, Blues, Dixie, Jazz, Hot Cha Cha and Boogie Woogie, which surely originates in the jungle. We sometimes wonder whether this is the Negro's revenge.
(Historian Dominic Sandbrook read this *Daily Mail* editorial about Rock and Roll in *50s Britannia: Rock and Roll Britannia,* BBC television, 2013)

ACTIVITIES . . .

1. List the three main challenges that Caribbean arrivals faced living in Britain.

2. What musical elements created Rock and Roll? How did it differ from Rockabilly?

3. How did Rock and Roll influence American culture? Why is this significant? How does this show cultural change?

4. What was the significance of Tommy Steele, and Cliff Richard & the Shadows? What was the significance of The Southlanders?

5. From Source A, list five facts about the typical dress code of the Teddy Boys.

6. According to Source B, what date did the Teddy Boy subculture start? What date did Rock and Roll change the subculture?

7. What comment did Source C give to show he was shocked when he first heard Little Richard?

8. According to Source D, why did the *Daily Mail* claim that 'Ragtime, Blues, Dixie, Jazz, Hot Cha Cha and Boogie Woogie ... surely originates in the jungle'?

EXTENDED WRITING

Using your imagination, write a letter of complaint to the *Daily Mail* about Rock and Roll. Say why their reference to the jungle is not acceptable. Say also why Rock and Roll is revolutionising Youth Culture for the first time.

Learning Objective: To understand the impact Black Migrants had on the NHS

In April 1956 London Transport began to recruit workers from Barbados to work on the buses and the underground. Within 12 years, this organisation had 3,787 Bajans working for them. Incidentally, the Bajan government even published an information booklet for Bajans warning them of what to expect of life in Britain. The booklet was called *Information Booklet For Intending Emigrants To Britain.*

Other recruitment programmes in the Caribbean and Guyana brought people to work for British Rail and the National Health Service. Thus, Black male migrants worked on the railways, underground, buses, factory work and the Post Office. Black female migrants worked in hospitals, cafes, and as bus conductors. By 1958 there were around 125,000 Caribbeans living in Britain. Brixton in South London became the unofficial capital of Black Britain.

Black workers made a big impact on London Transport and British Rail. However, the biggest impact of all was on the National Health Service. BBC television even aired a documentary in 2016 called *Black Nurses: The Women Who Saved the NHS.* The documentary told of the racism the Black nurses endured from White patients and administrators, to winning respect, to some eventually gaining recognition. Black nurses found an effective way to advance their careers. They specialised as midwives.

Daphne Steele (sister of Carmen Munroe, page 64) came to Britain from Guyana. She became a matron in St Winifred's, a West Yorkshire Hospital, in 1964. She was the first Black woman to become a matron. Dr David Pitt came from Grenada to study medicine at Edinburgh. Beginning as a GP in the 1940s, he became President of the British Medical Association in 1985. Jamaican Karlene Davis, trained as a midwife in 1967 and became General Secretary of The Royal College of Midwives in 1997. The first Black female Trade Union leader in Britain, she transformed this organisation into a modern professional organisation. African American Dr Beverly Malone became General Secretary of The Royal College of Nurses in 2001. Ghanaian Dr Bernard Ribeiro worked as consultant general surgeon at Basildon Hospital in 1979 where he pioneered keyhole surgery. He became President of the Royal College of Surgeons in 2005.

Bringing the story up to date, a Black midwife, Professor Jacqui Dunkley-Bent, led the team that delivered Prince George and Princess Charlotte, children of the Duke and Duchess of Cambridge. Moreover, Dr Pitt became Baron Pitt of Hampstead, Dr Ribeiro is now Baron Ribeiro, of Achimota in the Republic of Ghana and of Ovington in the County of Hampshire, and Karlene Davis is now Dame Karlene Davis MBE. There is a portrait of her in the National Portrait Gallery.

Source A
You will find that the people in the United Kingdom are less inclined to join you in conversation than your own people in Barbados.
(*Information Booklet For Intending Emigrants To Britain,* quoted in Tony Sewell, *Keep On Moving: The Windrush Legacy,* p. 29)

My father had a brother in England ... When I got to his house, they didn't have a bath ... And I realised it was normal and I asked him ... "Where is your bath?" ... And he said ... "We go once a week to Caledonia Road baths" ... And I thought ... 'How could he live and not bathe?' ... You bathe twice a day minimum in Trinidad.
(Allyson Williams MBE, interviewed in *Black Nurses: The Women Who Saved the NHS*, BBC television, 2016)

Source C
24 per cent of the West Indians coming to Britain had professional or managerial experience, 46 per cent were skilled workers, 5 per cent semi-skilled and only 13 per cent unskilled manual workers.
(Tony Sewell, *Keep On Moving: The Windrush Legacy*, p. 35)

Source D
40,000 nurses and midwives from around the Commonwealth answered the call from "the Mother Country" to help build Nye Bevan's nascent National Health Service.
(Michael Hogan, *Black Nurses: The Women Who Saved the NHS is a story of courage and achievement in the face of adversity: review*, in *The Telegraph*, 24 November 2016)

Source E
How could the RCN want an American, an African American to run the most prestigious professional nursing trade union in the world?
(Dr Beverly Malone, quoted by Wikipedia, 2007)

ACTIVITIES . . .

1. List the jobs that Black men and Black women did in Britain.

2. What was the significance of Brixton?

3. What three industries did Black migrants have the biggest impact on?

4. Pick two of the following individuals and say why they are significant: Daphne Steel, David Pitt, Karlene Davis, Beverly Malone, Bernard Ribeiro, and Jacqui Dunkley-Bent.

5. What can we learn about the cultural differences between the Caribbean and England from Sources A and B?

6. How can Source C be used to challenge the idea that Black migrants were just poor and backward peasants?

7. What does Source D tell us about the scale of the impact that Commonwealth nurses had on the NHS?

8. What impression does Source E give of the RCN (Royal College of Nurses)?

17

Learning Objective: To understand how competition and resentment between Black Migrants and the Host Community led to anti-Black Violence

After the influx of Black people into the British cities, there were racial conflicts with local Whites. These conflicts culminated in anti-Black racial violence in the summer of 1958. The Black population competed with Whites for housing, employment and even women. Many Whites objected to Blacks moving into what they saw as 'their' areas, taking 'their' jobs, and dating 'their' women.

White landlords often refused to RENT property to Blacks. They would place adverts that read: 'No Blacks, No Irish, No dogs.' In response, Black people BOUGHT houses instead. They raised money using an old credit and saving scheme from Africa and the Caribbean called 'Pardna'. Each week, a large group of Blacks paid money into this scheme but only one person would withdraw all the money and buy a house. The following week, everyone paid into the scheme. Another person withdrew all the money and bought a house. They continued to run 'Pardna' until everyone bought their own house.

Resentment against Black people exploded in the hot summer of 1958 in Notting Hill, West London, and in Nottingham. Angry Whites abused Black and White couples. Even White women who dated Black men were beaten up. Some were accused of being prostitutes. The Black men were said to have ran brothels. As the race riots progressed, Blacks faced terror as gangs of White youths threw petrol bombs through their windows. Many of the gangs were Teddy Boys. This phase of violence lasted for six weeks.

In May 1959, nine months after the riots, Teddy Boys in Notting Hill killed a Black man. Kelso Cochrane, an Antiguan carpenter, was stabbed to death. This was the first acknowledged racial killing and made headline news. A massive 1200 people turned up for the funeral, both Black and White. British Pathé news televised the funeral. However, no one was ever arrested for the murder. The Black Community felt that nobody cared. They did not feel protected by the police.

In response to this violence, Claudia Jones, the great Black civil rights activist, started Carnival to highlight Black culture and to bring Black and White together. Held at St Pancras Hall in 1959, Carnival eventually moved to Notting Hill in the mid 1960s.

Source A

Something new and ugly raises its head in Britain ... racial violence. An angry crowd of youths chases a Negro into a greengrocer's shop, while police reinforcements are called up to check the riot, one of many that have broken out here in a few days. The injured victim, a Jamaican, is taken to safety. But the police have not been able to reach all the trouble spots so promptly ... The most disturbing feature of the riots is the suspicion that not all the troublemakers are locals. Some of the gangs who break windows or throw bottles or burning torches have arrived by car.
(British Pathé news, *Notting Hill: Shameful Episode,* 1958)

Source B

There was ... a pitched battle, in Powis Terrace ... between black men, policemen, white yobbos and Teddy Boys ... the street was alight, except for fires and ... Molotov Cocktails ... the situation had

become so bad that black men used to come from surrounding areas like Paddington and Brixton and Shepherd's Bush ... knowing the whites were going to hit a particular street.
(Ivan Weekes, interviewed in Mike Phillips & Trevor Phillips, *Windrush,* 1998, p. 175)

Source C
I was away to [the] Pictures, and [on] my return, I found that my house and the windows had been smashed to pieces.
(Nigerian university student, interviewed in Notting Hill just after the riots, 1958)

Source D
They [Teddy Boys] chose streets where only a few black people were seen, and they attacked in the ratio of six to one, the Police generally took little notice of these attacks, whose frequency of violence steadily increased.
(*Manchester Guardian* quoted in Peter Fryer, *Staying Power,* p. 378)

Source E
Before the riots I was British – I was born under the Union Jack. But the race riots made me realise who I am and what I am. They turned me into a staunch Jamaican.
(Baron Baker, interviewed in Tony Sewell, *Keep On Moving: The Windrush Legacy,* p. 52)

ACTIVITIES . . .

1. Copy this out and join the Cause to the Consequence

Cause	Consequence
Blacks moved in to Notting Hill, so	Claudia Jones started St Pancras Carnival
Most of the Black Migrants were men, so	1200 people attended his funeral
Landlords refused to rent to Blacks, so	White gangs destroyed Black owned property
Blacks bought houses, Whites rented, so	Blacks used 'Pardna' to buy houses
Cochrane's killing made national news, so	This increased competition for White women
Black White relations needed to improve, so	This increased competition for jobs and housing

2. According to Sources A and B, what types of violent acts did Blacks face in Notting Hill? What is the evidence that the violence was planned? Where is the evidence that the Black response was planned?

3. What did Source C do for a living? How might his status have been different from other Notting Hill Blacks?

4. According to Source D, how did the Teddy Boys select who was going to be attacked?

5. Compare Source A (a government approved source) with Source D (a newspaper). According to these sources, what did the police do about this anti-Black violence? In your opinion, why do you think the sources differ?

EXTENDED WRITING

What do you think Source E meant? Give three reasons why Black Migrants may have originally been proud to be British. Give three reasons why this pride in Britishness ended in 1958 and 1959. How do you think you would have felt as a Migrant during that period?

Learning Objective: To understand how Black Britain's leading civil rights fighter created what evolved into Europe's largest street party

Claudia Jones was born in Trinidad in 1915. She moved to New York, Harlem, with her parents at the age of 8. She became an active member of the American Communist Party. Their ethos was social equality and they offered a voice for those fighting for Black civil rights. By 1948, Claudia was the editor of Negro Affairs for the party's paper the *Daily Worker*. She had also evolved into an accomplished speaker on human and civil rights.

However, in 1948, she was arrested for her political activities and sentenced to the first of four periods in prison. Finally, following a year in the Alderson Federal Reformatory for Women, she was deported. She was refused entry into Trinidad and in 1955 was granted asylum in England.

In London, Claudia Jones became the leader of the emerging Black equal rights movement. She spent her remaining years working with London's African-Caribbean community. In 1958, she founded and edited *The West Indian Gazette and Afro-Asian Caribbean News*. It was the only newspaper printed in London for the Black community at that time. The paper provided a forum to discuss civil rights and equal opportunities for Black people in Britain. The paper campaigned against anti-Black racism in housing, education, and employment.

Claudia Jones legacy was undoubtedly Carnival, which she helped launch on 30 January 1959 as an annual showcase for Caribbean talent. These early celebrations were held in halls and were epitomised by the slogan: 'A people's art is the genesis of their freedom'.

The world's largest annual carnival is held in Trinidad and Tobago and is rooted in Calypso and Soca music. Carnival spread to many other islands, where the tradition fused with the local cultures. Trinidad and Tobago's centrepiece event was copied by many cities around the world, including London's Notting Hill Carnival. The Rio Carnival in Brazil is the world's second biggest carnival.

London's Caribbean-themed Carnivals evolved over many years:

1959	Claudia Jones and her committee led the St Pancras Town Hall Carnival, Euston. The BBC broadcasted a 30-minute portion of it at 10.45pm, 30 January, entitled *Trinidad Comes to Town*.
1960	Claudia Jones and her committee led the Seymour Hall Carnival, Marble Arch. Another indoor show was held at the Kensington Town Hall.
1961	Claudia Jones and her committee led the Carnival at the Lyceum Theatre, Covent Garden. British Movietone partially filmed this event.
1962	Claudia Jones and her committee led the Seymour Hall Carnival, Marble Arch.
1963	Claudia Jones and her committee led the Seymour Hall Carnival, Marble Arch. Another event took place in Manchester.
1964	Rhaune Laslett a Social Worker of White and Native American heritage, held a diverse and multicultural Notting Hill Fair and Pageant. This moved the event to Notting Hill, West London, and made it an outdoor party.

It would be unfair for me not to tell you that we have still another determination, that is, to make the ...
Caribbean Carnival an annual event
(Claudia Jones wrote this in *A Souvenir of the Caribbean Carnival 1959*)

Connor, the director, had told the Jamaica Gleaner, "We want to make it as much like the Port of Spain
one as possible."
(Ray Funk, *Notting Hill Carnival: Mas and the mother country* in *Caribbean Beat Magazine*,
November/December 2009)

It ... featured among other things the Mighty Terror singing the calypso "Carnival at St Pancras", a
Caribbean Carnival Queen beauty contest, the Trinidad All Stars and Hi-fi steel bands dance troupe and
a Grand Finale Jump-Up by West Indians who attended the event.
(About the 1959 St Pancras event from the *Notting Hill Carnival* website)

1963: From Beauty to Masquerade
The event occurred again at Seymour Hall and then to Manchester. The programme shifted from the
beauty contest to a carnival masquerade costume competition.
(About the 1963 Seymour Hall event from the *Notting Hill Carnival* website)

Don't rain on our parade! Notting Hill Carnival kicks off as the sun comes out for 1 million revellers at
Europe's biggest street party
(*Daily Mail* headline, 25 August 2013)

ACTIVITIES . . .

1. What was Claudia Jones doing in 1948? What skills did she learn that would be useful to her later career? Why did she leave the United States?

2. What are the two most important carnivals in the world?

3. Read Source B, why did Edric Connor want to make the event (in Euston) as much like the one in Port of Spain (in Trinidad)?

4. Source C mentions a 'Caribbean Carnival Queen beauty contest'. Why do you think this was important, especially at that time?

5. Where is the evidence in Source D that the Seymour Hall event was getting even closer to Carnival as we know it today?

6. According to Source E, what is the significance of London Carnival? How many people were expected to come to it in 2013?

7. Compare all the sources A to E. In YOUR opinion, which source gave the most important information about Carnival and say why.

CLASS EIGHT: ORIGIN OF MERSEY BEAT AND BRITISH RHYTHM & BLUES 1958 - 1965

Learning Objective: How African American music created the British Beat and Rhythm & Blues explosion

White merchant seamen brought African American Rhythm & Blues and Soul records from America to the British port cities: Liverpool, Belfast, Newcastle. These Blues and Soul records brought a new vein of life to British music in the late 1950s and the 1960s.

Many Whites who listened to this imported music were inspired to copy it. These White musicians, led by the Beatles, created the Merseybeat or 'Beat' scene in Liverpool. Other musicians, led by the Rolling Stones, created a British Rhythm and Blues scene across the UK. British Beat and Rhythm & Blues music achieved global importance. British bands sold their music all over the world, even to White America, and topped the charts.

Merseybeat started in Liverpool. The Liverpool scene centred on a small club called the Cavern. Amongst the performers were The Beatles, Cilla Black, The Undertakers (known for *The Mashed Potato*), The Searchers (*Sweets for my Sweet*), The Swinging Blue Jeans (*Your no Good*) and The Merseybeats (*I think of You*). Liverpool is important for another reason. It is the home of the oldest continuous Black Community in Britain from well before 1948. Black people have lived in Liverpool as a continuous community since the Eighteenth Century.

Marketed as an anti-Beatle band, the Rolling Stones were the leading Rhythm and Blues band. Influenced by African American bluesmen such as Muddy Waters, the Rolling Stones even took their name from the lyrics of a Muddy Waters song. Mick Jagger, the lead singer, copied many of his dance moves from James Brown. The other Rhythm and Blues bands included Them (from Belfast), The Animals (from Newcastle), The Hollies (from Manchester) and The Who (from West London).

Source A

In Liverpool, a new music scene was about to explode with a new distinctive sound, thanks to the city's port. Ernie Sealey was a teenager when he bought the latest thrilling sound from America off a sailor who worked on the transatlantic ships between Liverpool and New York ... This was Soul and Rhythm & Blues, heavier and more raw than anything experienced before. Kids all over Liverpool were inspired to pick up guitars and copy the sound. Beat Music had arrived.
(Twiggy in *The People's History of Pop, Episode 1*, BBC television, 2016)

Source B

Woodbine was not ambitious; The Beatles were, and like most young people, they were takers and triers. The Trinidadian helped guide them through their formative musical years.
(Yasmin Alibhai-Brown and James McGrath, *Lord Woodbine: The forgotten sixth Beatle*, in *The Independent*, 30 June 2010)

Source C

The band's [i.e. Rolling Stones] policy is to play authentic Chicago rhythm and blues music, using outstanding exponents of the music such as [African Americans] Howlin' Wolf, Muddy Waters, Bo Diddley, Jimmy Reed, etc.
(Rolling Stones, Letter to BBC, January 1963)

Source D

There were a lot of us White girls around trying to sound Black. Loads of us wanted to sound Black because there was nobody inspiring who was White.
(Julie Driscoll, soul singer interviewed in *Soul Britannia: Episode 1, I Feel Good*, BBC television, 2006)

Source E

I wanted to sing like Ray and I did for a while. I used to just ape Ray Charles on stage, a lot of us did.
(Eric Burdon, lead singer of the Animals interviewed in *Soul Britannia: Episode 1, I Feel Good*, BBC television, 2006)

Source F

We really thought that when we went to America and played them that music it wouldn't work because it was their music. We didn't realise that the White [American] kids had never heard that music.
(Bill Wyman, bass player of Rolling Stones interviewed in *Dancing in the Streets: Crossroads*, BBC television, 1995)

ACTIVITIES . . .

1. How did African American music get to the British port cities?

2. (i) What was the 'Beat' music scene? What was the British Rhythm & Blues scene? (ii) Why did these musical forms achieve global importance?

3. Apart from music, why else is Liverpool important to Black British history?

4. List three examples that show how African Americans influenced the Rolling Stones.

5. According to Source A, why did Rhythm & Blues and Soul make such an impact on Liverpudlian youngsters?

6. According to Source B, why was Trinidadian Lord Woodbine important to the Beatles?

7. Referring to Sources C, D, and E, what impression did White British musicians have of African American musicians?

EXTENDED WRITING

Write an article for a business magazine called *British Bands Conquer America!* Using Source F, explain in detail why British musicians became so successful with White Americans. Explain also the business reasons why African American musicians were annoyed by the success of British musicians.

Learning Objective: What was the second musical culture that Black Migrants brought to the UK?

Ska was a style of music that originated in Jamaica in 1959. It was a Jamaican variation of African American Rhythm & Blues, and Soul. The African American shuffle beat influenced Jamaican musicians. Ska bands had guitarists, saxophonists, trumpeters, bass players and drummers. Ska is a musical style but also refers to a dance that goes along with it. The dance was later called the Skank or Skanking. Ska replaced the dominance that Trinidadian music had in Jamaica.

African American music was popular in 1950s Jamaica. Jamaicans particularly liked James Brown, Ray Charles and BB King. Jamaican DJs played records by these artists to 'sound clash' against other DJs to prove who was the best. Sound systems such as Coxsone Dodd, Duke Reid's The Trojan, and Prince Buster became well known sound clash DJs. Eventually, some of these DJs became important recording artists. Influenced by the African American records that they sound clashed with, they created Ska. Ska helped to build a sense of national pride in Jamaican cultural identity.

Jamaican migrants brought Ska music to England, where it would be played alongside Trinidadian Calypso. In Britain, Ska became popular with younger Blacks. Calypso was preferred by older Blacks. Ska also influenced a new British youth subculture called Mod (short for 'Modernists'). The Mods adopted this music as their own.

Prince Buster was the leading Ska artist. His biggest hit was called *Madness*. Other important groups and solo artists included The Maytals, Eric Morris and Jimmy Cliff. Interestingly, one of the Ska bands was led by a Chinese Jamaican: Byron Lee. When Jamaica became independent from British rule in 1962, the Jamaican government promoted Ska as the music of independence. Millie Small's *My Boy Lollipop* was a Ska version of an African American Doo Wop song *My Girl Lollypop*. Selling over seven million copies, it is still Jamaica's bestselling Ska song of all times reaching Number 1 in the British Charts.

By around 1966, Ska evolved into a new form of Jamaican music called Rocksteady. By around 1968, Rocksteady evolved into a new form of Jamaican music called Reggae. Thus, Ska is the parent of Rocksteady and the grandparent of Reggae.

Source A
Exclusivity has always been a major component in sound system Jamaica, the way that a given sound system was able to retain loyalty in a very competitive field. And in Jamaica, a way of hoping to preserve this would be to scratch off the label so that no one could identify what the song was actually called. No rival sound could identify what song you had.
(David Kats, *Jamaican Sound System Culture,* published on YouTube 2010)

Source B
I listened to people from abroad, who we call foreigners, like Smiley Louis, Sam Cook, Ray Charles, Fats Domino and they were very inspiring ... when I started out in Jamaica, I was inspired by music from ... Cuba ... then R & B mainly from New Orleans, then Jazz ... and Blues, Country and then when I came to the UK, I was opened up to a whole other world of music again.
(Jimmy Cliff, *Interview with Sarfraz Manzoor,* published on YouTube 2012)

Source C

There are four basic steps to the Ska: The first step is to keep the beat with the upper half of the body, bowing forward with a straight back and a slight bend in both knees. At the first bow, the arms extend to the sides. At the second bow, the arms cross in front. The body straightens up in-between the change of arms, from one position to the other. Basic step number two is practically the same as step number one but with the addition of a side step ... Step number three is, once again, very similar. Only the arms change ... Finally, our fourth basic step – now this is perhaps the most energetic of all ... and it's called 'rowing'... It is either done facing your partner or beside your partner ... Ska is as easy as that!
(Tony Verity in *This is Ska!* Jamaica Broadcasting Company, 1964)

Source D

The original song, "My Girl Lollypop", was written by Robert Spencer of the doo-wop group The Cadillacs ... Although not involved in writing the song, Levy and alleged gangster Johnny Roberts listed themselves as the song's authors.
(*My Boy Lollipop,* Wikipedia page)

ACTIVITIES . . .

1. Why might the birth of Ska music have been a problem for Trinidadian musicians that worked in Jamaica?

2. In three steps, show how African American music evolved into Ska.

3. How did Ska come to England? What impact did it have in England?

4. Draw a time line of the key facts from the 1950s to 1968.

5. According to Source A, how did Jamaican DJs build an audience that was loyal to them?

6. Jimmy Cliff was an important Ska musician (Source B). What musical forms influenced him?

7. Who do you think Source C was aimed at?

8. Robert Spencer was the African American musician mentioned in Source D. (i) Explain what stopped him from making big money from his original *My Girl Lollypop*. (ii) Explain why these types of business practices were a problem for Black musicians.

Learning Objective: How Civil Rights Struggles improved the lives and opportunities for Black Britons

When Blacks came to Britain in the Calypso Years, the biggest problems they faced was getting accommodation, finding well paid work, and avoiding Teddy Boys and other racists. Thus, Black Migrants often lived in poor accommodation, worked long hours for low pay, and were often beaten and abused by racists.

By the Rocksteady and Reggae Years (1966-1978), a generation of Black children were now born in Britain. Their main problems were getting decent quality schooling, finding work, and avoiding harassment from the Police. Thus, Black Britons often experienced poor schooling, no employment, and were picked on by the Police. Reggae music spoke to the poverty and hopelessness that Black British youth felt in the 1970s.

There were many Civil Rights Struggles that Black people fought to improve their treatment in Britain. We shall look at three of them: The Bristol Bus Boycott of 1963, the Oxford Street Campaign in the mid 60s, and The Mangrove Nine in 1969-1970.

Paul Stephenson, a Black youth worker, led the Bristol Bus Boycott of 1963. At the time, the Bristol Bus Company refused to employ Black drivers or conductors. Stephenson, inspired by Dr Martin Luther King in the United States, called on people to boycott the Bus Company as a protest. The Boycott went on for four months. It brought media attention to the 'Colour Bar' in Britain. The Bristol Bus Company, under pressure from the boycott and the media, finally agreed to hire Black workers. Moreover, the Labour Party agreed with Stephenson and eventually passed *The Race Relations Act of 1965* to undermine the Colour Bar.

Jocelyn Barrow led a campaign against the Colour Bar in Oxford and Regent Street, Central London. Black people at the time were not allowed to work in the shop fronts serving customers. Employers felt that White people would not want to buy clothes or food handled by Black people. They were happy to employ Blacks if they were not visible to the public. This caused an outrage in the Black Community that Barrow addressed. She was the General Secretary of the Campaign Against Racial Discrimination in 1964 and the group lasted until 1967. They were inspired by Dr King's visit to London in 1964. The Campaign Against Racial Discrimination influenced the government to pass the *Race Relations Act of 1968.*

The Mangrove restaurant in Notting Hill, was a central meeting place for Black Community spokesmen, authors, artists, and musicians. One attendee was the brilliant scholar C. L. R. James. The restaurant was also the informal office for the Notting Hill Carnival. However, the police raided it twelve times between 1969 and 1970. Blacks protested this which ended in violence. Nine Blacks were arrested including Frank Critchlow and Darcus Howe. The media called these people 'The Mangrove Nine'. However, at the trial, all nine were freed. This changed the nine into celebrities in the Black Community who stood up against police hostility and racism.

Source A

Since I come 'ere I never met a single English person who 'ad any colour prejudice. Once, I walked the whole length of a street looking for a room, and everyone told me that he or she 'ad no prejudice against coloured people. It was the neighbour who was stupid.

(Alvin Gladstone Bennett quoted in James Ferguson, *When London was the place,* on *Caribbean Beat* website, January/February 2016)

I was committed to what Luther King was doing [in the US] so I decided we would do something here [i.e. Bristol] about it because this was a de facto *segregationist city.*
(Paul Stephenson reminiscing about the Bus Boycott, in *Jamaicans in Bristol's fight against racism,* YouTube, 2 March 2010)

To get Black people in shops we actually had to get the cooperation of one of the key persons in the Oxford and Regent Street Traders Association. And this person said to me ... "If you can find me four pretty Black girls ... I will employ them and then my colleagues will follow."
(Dame Jocelyn Barrow reminiscing about the Oxford Street campaign, in *Black British Civil Rights Dame Jocelyn Barrow,* YouTube, 17 February 2011)

It has been for some time now that Black people have been caught up in complaining to police about police, complaining to magistrates about magistrates, complaining to judges about judges, complaining to politicians about politicians. We have become the shepherds of our destinies as from today.
(Darcus Howe, 1969 speech, in *Mangrove Nine 1970's - Darcus Howe, Frank Critchlow, etc ...,* YouTube, 26 March 2012)

ACTIVITIES . . .

1. How were life and opportunities SIMILAR for Blacks in the Calypso Years compared with the Rocksteady and Reggae Years? How were they DIFFERENT?

2. What was the Colour Bar?

3. Copy and complete this table:

Black Civil Rights Fighter	What did they do?	What Law did they influence?
Paul Stephenson		
Jocelyn Barrow		

4. How did Frank Critchlow and Darcus Howe become celebrities in the Black Community?

EXTENDED WRITING

Using Sources B, C, and D, other information, and your imagination, write an account of ONE of these civil rights struggles from the first-person perspective of Paul Stephenson, Jocelyn Barrow, or Darcus Howe.

Learning Objective: To show another example of how Black culture influenced a White youth subculture

The Mod movement was a White British working-class subculture. The subculture became dominant in the early 1960s. The Mods wanted to present a clean, sharp, modern style. Mod life centred on scooters, fashion, and music. One Mod band was particularly influential: The Beatles.

The male dress code was sharp, slick, and aspirational. Men wore narrow ties, suits with narrow lapels and pork pie hats. Chic Italian and French styles influenced the fashion. Kingston Jamaican styles, brought by Caribbean arrivals, also influenced Mod fashion. Prince Buster was a major style icon.

Not all of Mod fashion was Black influenced, however. Teenage girls began to join the Mod culture, which was previously male dominated. Mary Quant, a Welsh fashion designer, had a huge influence on female Mod styles. A British fashion icon, she originated the mini skirt.

The Mods listened to the coolest music of the time. They loved African American Rhythm and Blues. They also loved Jamaican Ska. However, the Mods called the Jamaican music 'Blue Beat' as opposed to Ska. Blue Beat was actually the name of a record label that made Ska records. Jimmy James & The Vagabonds, a Ska and Soul septet from Kingston, Jamaica, became a favourite of the scooter-riding Mod scene. They successfully toured Britain where they performed to Mod audiences.

By 1965, one branch of the Mod subculture evolved into Northern Soul. This was the first all night clubbing scene in the working-class Northern British cities. Starting at the Twisted Wheel club in Manchester, the scene spread to Droitwich, Wolverhampton, Blackpool, Stoke-on-Trent, and Wigan. Fuelled by stimulant drugs, thousands of young White Mods came to dance at this cool underground scene. The DJs played high energy African American Soul. They even visited America to buy these cool Black records.

Source A
In 1958, a small group of tailor's sons in East London adopted a smooth and sophisticated look, a combination of Italian and French styles of the period. They had Italian suits with narrow lapels impeccably tailor-made for themselves, and wore them with pointed-collar shirts. The shoes ... were hand-made winkle-pickers, so named because of their extremely pointed toes which so closely resembled the pins used to pick the meat out of a type of snail called a periwinkle. To top off the look, Mods wore their hair short and neat, following the lead of French film stars.
(Melissa M. Casburn, *A Concise History of the British Mod Movement*, no date given)

Source B
That cool Caribbean clothing had arrived in the same working-class areas of London, Notting Hill, Brixton, Tottenham, as the Mods lived in. With their trousers an inch or two above their shoes, and their trilbies at an acute angle, these Jamaican dudes became role models for White boys who wanted to look like Rude Boys ... In the early 60s, Mods were adopting, not just the fashions from Jamaica, but also the new music from that island known as Ska.
(*Soul Britannia: Episode 1, I Feel Good*, BBC television, 2006)

The music [i.e. Ska] ... was played exclusively in discotheques, because BBC radio simply ignored the music.
(Sebastian Clarke, *Jah Music*, p. 140)

Originally, mod was about modern jazz (listened to by the modernists), but as we entered the 1960s, it was R&B, soul and Jamaican ska--the music of choice for the clubs of the day, augmented by the beat bands of the day who often re-interpreted the imported soul grooves, creating the beat group sound of the mid-60s.
(*What is Mod Music?* from *Mod Culture* website)

Our Mod following was huge, I wouldn't even say large. It was huge. Thousands. When we did places like Brighton Pier ... they were closing the place at seven o' clock: 'No more, no more, no more.' It was huge.
(Jimmy James, lead singer of Jimmy James & The Vagabonds, interviewed in *Soul Britannia: Episode 1, I Feel Good*, BBC television, 2006)

ACTIVITIES . . .

1. What were the three most important things in Mod life?

2. From which countries did Mod male styles originate?

3. Who was the biggest influence on Mod female dress? What did she pioneer?

4. Explain how 'Blue Beat' got this name.

5. How was the Northern Soul scene SIMILAR to what happens today? How was it DIFFERENT from what happens today?

6. Using Sources A and B, give details of the Mod male dress code.

7. According to Source C, 'BBC radio ... ignored the music'. Explain why this may have INCREASED its popularity with the Mods.

8. Using Sources D and E, suggest how music may have helped to reduce hatred against Blacks.

Learning Objective: What was the third musical culture that Black Migrants brought to the UK?

Rocksteady was a style of Jamaican music that evolved from Ska in around 1966. The sound was slower with a calm and relaxed mood. The bass sound was fatter and the drums were more prominent. The singing style was more elegant than Ska and borrowed sophisticated harmonies from African American Soul groups. Some of the song lyrics were more romantic than Ska. Other lyrics were more political or about social issues. In total, some say that Rocksteady was the Golden Age of Jamaican music. Rocksteady was also the mother of Reggae.

Rocksteady would typically be sung by vocal harmony trios such as The Paragons, The Heptones, and the Wailers. There were also solo artists like Desmond Dekker, Derek Morgan and John Holt.

Many artists sang about love and culture. Another theme was the Jamaican Rude Boys, a Jamaican term used to describe gangsters. Desmond Dekker's *007 (Shanty Town)*, recorded in 1966, described these Rude Boys. Derrick Morgan's song *Tougher than Tough* is on the same topic.

Following Jamaica's independence in 1962, Kingston, the capital of Jamaica, attracted more people than jobs. The lack of work contributed to a rise in violence. Many young men joined gangs and became Rude Boys. As poverty and violence spread throughout the country, Rocksteady songs became less about love and romance, and more about crime and Jamaica's social problems. Some songs defended the Rude Boys. Other songs were against them. Some historians have compared this music to the more recent African American Gangsta Rap.

During this time, many Rocksteady artists left Jamaica to live and tour overseas. Consequently, the music was brought to other countries such as Canada, Belgium and Britain. Black Migrants in Britain bought these records as well as their children born in Britain. White British youth also listened to and bought Rocksteady records, such as the Skinheads and the Mods. In fact, the Skinhead look was particularly influenced by Desmond Dekker. His 1968 record, *Israelites,* topped the British charts in March 1969.

Punk Rock band, Blondie, and the pop band, Atomic Kitten, both covered The Paragons' classic 1967 Rocksteady hit *The Tide Is High*. This highlights the popularity of Rocksteady and its undeniable influence on other music and subcultures that followed.

Source A
Ask any Jamaican musician and they'll tell you the rocksteady days were the best days of Jamaican music.
(Derrick Harriott, a Jamaican record producer and musician, quoted in *Rocksteady*, Wikipedia page)

Source B
Dekker had always worn his hair very short, like the American crew cut, and wore short jackets and short trousers. The skinheads, white kids affecting the attire and cultural style of Desmond Dekker, then came into being. Like the Mods in imitation of Prince Buster.
(Sebastian Clarke, *Jah Music*, p. 148)

Source C
As a teenager, it was all the Ska stuff ... that was the era – '69, '70. All those great records coming through, the Desmond Dekker's and stuff but also, we used to go down Lewisham Market and get the Jamaican Ska stuff as it came in.
(Gary Bushell, a Skinhead interviewed in *2-Tone Britain*, Channel 4 television, 2004)

Source D
You're brought here for gun-shooting, ratchet using and bomb-throwings
Now tell me Rude Boys
What have you to say for yourselves?

Your honour, Rudies don't fear
Rudies don't fear, no boys, Rudies don't fear (x2)
Rougher than rough
Tougher than tough
Strong like lion
We are iron
(Derrick Morgan, *Tougher than Tough*, 1966)

ACTIVITIES . . .

1. What were the musical elements that distinguished Rocksteady from Ska?

2. Name two Rocksteady solo artists. Name two Rocksteady groups.

3. In what ways did the lyrics of Desmond Dekker's *007 (Shanty Town)* and Derrick Morgan's song *Tougher than Tough* reflect social realities of the time?

4. Give examples of how Rocksteady left influences around the world.

5. Do you think that Source A is a factual statement or do you think it is just Derrick Harriott's opinion? Explain your answer.

6. Read Source B. Is it likely that one individual can change the fashion of a whole group of people or do you think Sebastian Clarke has over simplified the story? Explain your answer.

7. Source C uses the term 'Ska'. However, he mentions the dates 1969 and 1970. Do you think he is really describing Ska music or is he describing Rocksteady?

EXTENDED WRITING

Write a newspaper article about Rocksteady music called *Rocksteady: Great music or murder music?* You must: (i) Discuss whether lyrics such as Source D encourage violence or is just describing violence. (ii) Say how this is SIMILAR TO Gangsta Rap and DIFFERENT FROM Gangsta Rap.

Learning Objective: Why was Enoch Powell such a controversial figure?

Enoch Powell was the Member of Parliament (MP) who represented Wolverhampton, in the West Midlands. In 1962, he became the Minister for Health and therefore controlled the National Health Service (NHS). To build up the NHS, he wanted nurses and doctors from the Caribbean and India to come to Britain. However, in 1968 he changed his views.

In April 1968 Powell made a famous rabble-rousing speech to a Birmingham audience. He strongly criticised Black and Brown people from the Commonwealth countries coming to live in Britain. The Commonwealth was a new name for the countries once ruled by the British Empire. Moreover, he did not want the government to approve the *Race Relations Act of 1968* which was being discussed in Parliament at that time.

He said that White people who lived in Wolverhampton had complained to him about Black and Brown people moving into the area. Some complained that this led to overcrowding of maternity wards. One complained that Coloured people pushed excrement through an old White lady's letter box. In the climax of the speech, Powell predicted there would be violence. He said: "Like the Roman, I seem to see the River Tiber foaming with much blood." When the speech was reported by the media, and, at a time when people still remembered the Nottingham and the Notting Hill race riots, his words were electric. The media gave his speech a name: 'Rivers of Blood'.

Powell's speech inspired hatred against Black and Brown people all over the country. People wrote 110,000 letters to Powell, mostly to agree with him. Only 2,300 of those letters disapproved of what he said. Two thousand White workers (dock workers and porters) stopped work and led a march to Parliament to support Powell. After the speech, there was a By Election to decide who was going to become the Member of Parliament for Smethwick, not too far from Wolverhampton. The Conservative Party won the By Election by agreeing with the anti-Black racists.

Powell's speech was a bad thing for Black (and Brown) people as White violence intensified. Many went in daily fear of their lives. Wooden crosses were burned outside Black homes all over the country. British racists who burned crosses copied the idea from terrorists in the United States called the Ku Klux Klan. A Jamaican in Smethwick was shot and killed. A Black boy in North Kensington was almost killed by a White gang, armed with iron bars and bottles.

Source A

During this time a Conservative health minister by the name of Enoch Powell welcomed Caribbean nurses to Britain. In fact, he actively went out to the Caribbean to beg women to join the new health service.
(Tony Sewell, *Keep On Moving: The Windrush Legacy,* p. 29)

Source B

In this country, in fifteen or twenty years' time, the Black man will have the whip hand over the White man.
(Enoch Powell, April 1968 speech)

Source C

I believe in plain talking, and Enoch Powell, without any question, said ... that he was speaking for thousands of Englishmen.
(Rene Webb quoted in Mike Phillips & Trevor Phillips, *Windrush*, 1998, pp. 242-3)

Source D

In the 1960s, there was a strong sense, among Black people of being under siege and feeling the need to fight for a place and a future in the country. This sense of being, under siege, was a recurring theme, also in the 1960s of white gangs targeting Black Communities.
(David Olusoga, *Black and British: A Forgotten History*, 2016, pp. 517-8)

ACTIVITIES . . .

1. How did Enoch Powell get large numbers of Black and Brown people to come and live in Britain in the 1960s?

2. When people used the term 'Commonwealth Immigrant', what did they mean by this?

3. List five facts about the 'Rivers of Blood' speech.

4. What is the evidence that many White people agreed with Powell?

5. Why was Powell's speech a bad thing for Black (and Brown) people?

6. Using Source B, why did Black people find Powell's use of the phrase 'whip hand' so offensive?

7. Using the Sources and other information, explain why Powell is a hero to some Whites, a threat to Blacks, and a fraud to Blacks. Present the information in a table.

Enoch Powell was a **hero**, because	Enoch Powell was a **threat**, because	Enoch Powell was a **fraud**, because

CLASS FOURTEEN: THE SKINHEAD SUBCULTURE

Learning Objective: To show a third example of how Black culture influenced a White youth subculture

The Skinheads were a tough, macho, working-class White subculture that came into existence in the late 1960s. Some people saw them as the younger brothers of the Teddy Boys. They derived their style from Black youths and from the Mods. Another influence on the Skinheads were the football boot boys who showed a strong and menacing presence at football matches.

The Skinheads took their style from the Mods (tight trousers) and from Black youths (shaved heads, mow hair suits, trousers worn an inch or two above their shoes, and white ankle socks). From this, they developed a dress code which included braces, Ben Sherman shirts with button down collars, Harrington jackets, Levi jeans, Dr Marten boots and shoes from America. The girls wore black patent shoes and two-toned skirts. Their identity was encoded in their appearance, music, and clothing. Their music of choice was from Jamaica: Rocksteady (and Reggae). Desmond Dekker was an early cultural icon for Skinheads.

The early Skinheads in the late 1960s were not prejudiced against Blacks. Black and White youth danced together to Rocksteady (and Reggae) on the dance floor. Skinhead culture became nationally popular in 1969, when the rock band Slade adopted the look as a marketing strategy.

However, this all changed in the 1970s. There were Asian immigrants coming to Britain in large numbers from India, Pakistan, and African countries: Kenya and Uganda. Some of the Skinheads targeted Asians moving into the inner cities. They would beat up Asians on sight. Moreover, the National Front, a racist Nazi inspired political movement, persuaded many Skinheads to join them. Racist Skinheads also targeted Blacks for violence.

Thus, Skinhead culture changed from a Rocksteady and Reggae influenced fashion statement in the late 60s, to a racist political movement urged on by the National Front in the 70s. From the late 70s till now, the Skinhead movement has continued to be divided into non-racist Traditional Skinheads on one hand, and Nazi Skinheads on the other.

Source A
Outside of West Indian communities, the biggest fans of Jamaican music were the Original Skinheads. Skinhead had formed out of the hard end of Mod, the football terrace boot boys and the Rude Boy style from Kingston, Jamaica ... the Skinheads took both their too short trousers and their close-cropped hair from West Indian immigrants.
(*2-Tone Britain,* Channel 4 television, 2004)

Source B
I think what you were witnessing there particularly among the young Skinheads and Mods ... was actually the first sign of the multicultural England because those Skinheads with their skanking dances and their Ska records were the first generation of White English kids to grow up with Black neighbours, Black schoolmates, to grow up with those rhythms.
(Robert Elms, interviewed in *UK Tribes,* television programme, 2006)

Source C
Skinheads were dancing to Ska music and just eating it up and I think that a lot of the British people probably wondered what was happening to their kids.
(Liz Mitchell, lead singer of Boney M, interviewed in *UK Tribes,* television programme, 2006)

Source D

I can remember sitting on over a bunch of skinheads and the[m] playing some U-Roy tune and I'm being totally amazed that these are guys who try and beat us up but they're listening to our music.
(Jazzy B, interviewed in Mike Phillips & Trevor Phillips, *Windrush,* 1998, p. 319)

Source E

Even though I was very ideologically involved with the National Front's credo, I was quite happy listening to [B]lack music. I loved soul music, I loved reggae music, I loved ska music. So ... you could call it a contradiction, it was certainly an oddity that we wanted an all-white culture and an all-white society, yet we were quite happy to imbibe this non-white culture.
(Joseph Pearce, former leader of the National Front's youth wing, interviewed in *The Story of Skinhead with Don Letts,* BBC television, 2016)

ACTIVITIES ...

1. What were the influences that created the Skinhead subculture?

2. How did the Skinheads dress?

3. Why did the camaraderie between the Skinheads and the Black Community break down in the 70s?

4. Read Source A. How do you think the Skinheads got their name?

5. Where is the evidence in Source B that shows Black people in Britain were seen less like foreigners and more like Britons?

6. Read Source C. Why do you think that 'a lot of the British people probably wondered what was happening to their kids'?

7. Source D mentions U-Roy, a Jamaican DJ. How does this source and Source E show how confused many Skinheads were by the 70s?

EXTENDED WRITING

Ian Stuart Donaldson, a Nazi Skinhead, said: "[P]art of being a Skinhead is to be a [White] Nationalist ... There's a lot said about Skinheads being started from Blacks in the East End but personally I don't think that's right at all, I mean I've heard [about] these Rude Boys ... but I don't consider them to be Skinheads anyway." Say whether you think he is right or wrong and support your answer with reasons.

CLASS FIFTEEN: THE REGGAE YEARS 1968 - 1978

Learning Objective: What was the fourth musical culture that Black Migrants brought to the UK?

Reggae is a style of music that originated in Jamaica in 1968. Evolving from Rocksteady, the bass sound was fatter, the drumming more intricate with the 'one drop' played on the bass drum, the sound more electric (as opposed to acoustic) and the whole vibe was more 'rootsy'. Reggae was also closely related to the pro-African and rebellious religious culture of Rastafari. By the 1970s, Reggae had become an international style recognised all over the world. It was particularly popular in the whole of the Caribbean, Britain, the United States, and in African countries.

Toots and the Maytals originally performed in the earlier Jamaican genres of Ska and Rocksteady. However, they started the new genre of Reggae with their 1968 hit single *Do the Reggay,* which gave the burgeoning genre its name. Toots and the Maytals appeared in the landmark reggae film *The Harder They Come* in 1972. However, the star of this film was another former Ska artist who reinvented himself as a Reggae artist: Jimmy Cliff. Known for the song *Many Rivers to Cross,* Jimmy Cliff became the first international star of Reggae.

The Wailers, led by Bob Marley, were originally a Rocksteady group. They reinvented themselves as a Reggae band and sold Reggae music across the globe. Though the group broke up at the height of their fame, Bob Marley eventually sold more than 20 million albums. He became the global face of Reggae and Jamaican music in every country in the world. He also did much to popularise Rastafari around the world.

Reggae influenced the Punk Rock subculture of the 70s. Punks, both in the United States and in Britain, listened to Reggae. For instance, The Roxy, a nightclub in Covent Garden, Central London, held the first British punk nights in 1976. However, the DJ at the club was a Black Rastafarian: Don (Rebel Dread) Letts. He played Reggae records to the Punk Rock crowd since there were no Punk records at that time to play.

Reggae music was identified as rebel music that was against 'The System'. Consequently, very little of this music was played on British radio or television. Young Blacks used to hold house parties called Blues Dances with huge sound systems to be able to hear Reggae. Moreover, wearing 'dreads' (as Rastas did) or spiked hair (as Punks did), identified you as a militant or an outlaw to British society. At the time, Black parents hoped their children did not embrace Rastafari. Similarly, White parents hoped their children did not embrace Punk Rock.

Source A
[T]he Blues Dance [meant] the turning of a single, two-roomed, or an entire house (abandoned or owned) into a simulated night club where the sound system would be hired to provide the music, and drinks and food ... sold at inflated prices.
(Sebastian Clarke, *Jah Music,* p. 148)

Source B
Punks are outcasts from society. So are the Rastas. So they are bound to defend what we defend.
(Bob Marley quoted in *Culture Clash: Bob Marley, Joe Strummer and the punky reggae party,* in *The Guardian,* 19 September 2014)

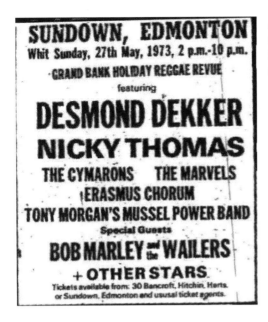

Advert for a concert in Edmonton, North London. This 1973 concert must have been something special. The performers included Reggae and Rocksteady musicians, Desmond Dekker, and Bob Marley.

Source C

More than a few classic rockers have poured the flavors of Jamaica into their music ... With the growing popularity of stars like Bob Marley and the Wailers, Peter Tosh and Jimmy Cliff in the '70s, all sorts of musicians — from hard rock titans to superstar folkies to punks — began to draw on reggae as a major influence.
(Bryan Wawzenek, *Top 10 Reggae Rock Songs* from the website *Ultimate Classic Rock,* no date given)

ACTIVITIES . . .

1. What were the musical elements of Reggae?

2. Why were Toots & the Maytals, Jimmy Cliff and Bob Marley significant? In your opinion, who was the most important of the three. Give a reason for your answer.

3. How did Punk Rockers get to hear Reggae? Why could they relate to it?

4. Except for Bob Marley, very little Reggae was played on British radio. How does this show a trend that goes back to the Ska era (see Source C, p. 29)?

5. Using Source A, show why (i) Blues Dances were a RESPONSE to anti-Black racism and (ii) CAUSED anti-Black racism.

6. Using Source B and other information, show why camaraderie developed between Punks and Rastas.

7. Using Source C and other information, demonstrate how Reggae became a music of global influence.

EXTENDED WRITING

Using the information here and your imagination, write a story called *Reggae Conquers the World* for a 1977 music magazine. The story should chart the origin and evolution of Reggae from nine years ago (1968) till now (1977).

Learning Objective: Why was the Notting Hill Carnival, 1976, of historic significance?

Notting Hill Carnival became the largest annual community event in the Black British calendar. In Trinidad, Carnival allowed people to dramatize their grievances against the people in power. Notting Hill Carnival, 1976, revived this idea of dramatizing grievances, but in a new and different way.

It included more than just Calypso and Steel Bands. It now included Soca, a new Trinidadian synthesis of Soul Music and Calypso, also Jamaican Reggae Sound Systems, in addition to other forms of music. There were stalls selling African Caribbean food and the size and scale of this outdoor party of music and dance got larger.

However, riots marred the third day of the Carnival, the Bank Holiday Monday. Black youths fought against the Police, throwing bricks, bottles, and Molotov cocktails. Several Police were stabbed. Ninety-Five Policemen were injured. The mass media reported on the violence. They reported on the Carnival in a very negative way. Black people were demonized in the Press.

Why did the anti-Police violence occur? Many of the rioters blamed the heavy-handed policing of the Carnival. Others saw the violence as payback for police harassment and continuous scrutiny of Black youth.

Source A

All the reports suggest that Scotland Yard was far too heavy-handed on Monday. It should not have sent 1500 uniformed men to police the Carnival in the Notting Hill area.
(Editorial in *Evening Standard,* quoted in Paul Gilroy, *There Ain't no Black in the Union Jack,* 1987, p. 96)

Source B

London's young blacks defeated the Metropolitan Police at the Notting Hill Carnival and major confrontations ... took place in Southall and in Birmingham.
(Paul Gilroy, *There Ain't no Black in the Union Jack,* 1987, p. 120)

Source C

Tempers were boiling among young black men over police use of the "sus" law, under which anybody could be stopped, searched and held, even if only suspected of planning a crime. Anticipating some trouble, 3,000 police officers turned up - ten times the amount of previous, relatively peaceful, events. This raised the tension, but what sparked the riot is still open to question. White fascist gangs were said to be at large. Police said it began after attempts to arrest a pickpocket. Whatever set it off, police officers were soon dodging a hail of bottles and a surging crowd.
(Emma Griffiths, *Remembering the Notting Hill riot,* BBC News website, 25 August 2006)

Source D

The West Indian Community emerged from the riots with a sense of pride. They had given the authorities a bloody nose and a strong message that they would no longer be treated without respect.
(Voice over, *Summer of Heat,* BBC television, 2016)

The violence at the 1976 Carnival received negative newspaper headlines.

Source E
It put an end to that idea that you can put people in their place, that you can treat people very badly, you can be overtly racist towards them and expect them to put up with it.
(Robert Elms, interviewed in *Summer of Heat*, BBC television, 2016)

ACTIVITIES . . .

1. What was the significance of Notting Hill Carnival to Black Britons?

2. How had the music changed since 1959?

3. What happened on the third day of the Carnival?

4. Copy this out and match the cause to the consequence

Cause
The Police expected trouble, so
The Police sent 1,500 officers, so
Black youth fought the police, so
The Press demonized Black youth, so

Consequence
Black youth felt more alienated
The Press demonized Black youth
Black youth saw this as baiting
1,500 officers were sent to the Carnival

5. Using Sources A, B, and other information, write 2 diary entries. Write the first diary entry from the point of view of a White policeman sent to police the Carnival and the violence that you faced. Write the second diary entry from the point of view of a Black youth who went to the Carnival and the police baiting that you faced.

6. Source C suggests 4 different theories why '[t]empers were boiling'. What were these theories?

7. Using Sources D and E, explain what good may have come out of the conflicts.

Learning Objective: To show a fourth example of how Black culture influenced a White youth subculture

Punk Rock was an anti-establishment subculture. It started in New York, USA, in the early 1970s. The music was harsh, confrontational, and had a raw guitar-heavy sound. Punk songs were short, often fast, with shouty rabble-rousing lyrics. Accompanying this new DIY sound was an anarchic DIY look: spiky hair, torn clothes, and safety pins.

Punk subculture came to Britain by 1975. During this time, there was high unemployment. Many White youths felt they had no future. Punk offered a new outlet for the White working-class and spoke to their anger and isolation.

The very first Punk disco in Britain had a Black DJ, Don Letts, playing Reggae music. Since Punk was so new and underground at that time, there wasn't any Punk Rock to play. So, Don Letts played the music he liked, which was Reggae. This appealed to the young White Punks who seemed to like the different musical sounds coming from Jamaica.

Leading Punk Rockers, Sex Pistols, and The Clash, were very much listeners of Reggae music. Bob Marley recorded *Punky Reggae Party* in 1977 to show the undeniable connection between Punk and Reggae music. Moreover, Punk groups began making music with a strong Reggae influence: The Police, The Stranglers, Chrissie Hynde & The Pretenders. In addition, one of the UK Punk bands, X Ray Spex, was led by Poly Styrene, a woman of English and Somalian heritage. Reggae influence also spread to US Punk music as well.

Reggae and Punk Rock came together in a British campaign called Rock Against Racism. Young musicians, Black and White came together in 1976 to object to racist statements made by British Rhythm and Blues musician, Eric Clapton. They also wanted to oppose the growth of the National Front, a racist Nazi inspired political movement. Over the next few years, the campaign involved getting Reggae, Punk, Pop, and Rock bands to stage joint concerts to mixed crowds of Black and White British youth. This exposed Black British youth to Punk Rock. It also exposed even more White youth to Reggae.

Source A
There was a lot of anticipation about 1977. Not only because of the stir that punk rock had created across the country and also in the Rasta circles the prophet Marcus Garvey had prophesised that when the 2 sevens clash, there would be chaos. As it turned out, there wasn't chaos in Jamaica but there sure was a lot of chaos in the United Kingdom.
(*The Clash*, BBC4 documentary, 2014)

Source B
My dad, a proud former punk rocker, tells me about the concerts he would go to in the 1970s, where they would play reggae music in between the punk acts. "There was no punk music recorded at the time," he explains.
(Charlie Brinkhurst-Cuff, *Why is the history of punk music so white?* from the Dazed website, 2016)

Poster advertising a 1978 Rock Against Racism event sponsored by the Anti-Nazi League. The bands featured on this poster were Tom Robinson Band (Punk) and Steel Pulse (Reggae).

Source C

"The bond was very simple", explains Peter Harris, a British reggae guitarist who played on Punky Reggae Party. "Blacks were getting marginalised." British Irish kids – like Rotten [lead singer of Sex Pistols] – and black youths were forced together because of signs on pub doorways that read "No Irish, No Blacks, No Dogs", which became the title of Rotten's autobiography.
(Dave Simpson, *Roots manoeuvre*, in *The Guardian*, 20 July 2007)

Source D

Like much in the way in the 60s bands used to cover contemporary R and B classics, we covered what was the latest record from Jamaica ... some of the guys from The Clash were in the riots.
(The Clash, interviewed in *Dancing in The Streets: No Fun*, BBC television, 1995)

Source E

It seemed as if every punk rocker started to walk with a skank.
(*Dancing in The Streets: No Fun*, BBC television, 1995)

ACTIVITIES . . .

1. Why did Punk Rock appeal to White working-class British youth?

2. Why were there no Punk records to play at the first Punk discos?

3. How did Black influence show itself in Punk music?

4. How did the Rock Against Racism campaign help ease tensions between Blacks and Whites?

5. Read Source A. How do you think The Clash came to know about the Honourable Marcus Garvey?

EXTENDED WRITING

Write a four-paragraph scholarly article called *Reggae influences on Punk Rock*. Use Source B as the basis for the first paragraph and add other information. Use Source C as the basis for the second paragraph and add other information. Use Source D as the basis for the third paragraph and add other information. Use Source E as the basis for the last paragraph and add other information.

Learning Objective: What was the first musical culture Black Britons invented in the UK?

Lovers Rock is a pioneering genre of music created out of the Sound Systems in South London. Beginning in the mid 1970s, Lovers Rock was the first music created by second generation Black British young people. They created a unique romantic sound that was not just a copy of Jamaican music. Prior to this, most Black music was brought to Britain from the Caribbean (or from the US).

Stylistically, Lovers Rock is about 75% Reggae and 25% Soul. The music recreated the vocal elegance of Rocksteady from nearly a decade earlier. In addition, Lovers Rock artists presented a more polished image that contrasted with the 'roots and culture' look of hard core Reggae artists.

This new sound appealed to women. In fact, women artists dominated the production of Lovers Rock records. Louisa Marks had a hit with *Caught You in a Lie* in 1975 when she was just 14. Other performers were Sandra Cross, Carol Thompson, and Jean Adebambo. At the height of Lovers Rock popularity, Janet Kay's hit single *Silly Games* reached number 2 in the UK Singles Chart in 1979.

Artists in Jamaica originally questioned if this new music was authentic. However, numerous well-established Jamaican artists also created music in this style. The most successful of these were Sugar Minott with his hit *Good Thing Going.* It peaked at Number 4 in the UK Singles Chart in 1981. Other Jamaican artists that performed in this genre were Dennis Brown, Gregory Isaacs, and later Freddie McGregor.

Outside of the Lovers Rock genre, second generation Black Britons produced two very high-quality Reggae bands during the late 1970s and early 80s: Steel Pulse and Aswad. They performed political music that expressed their experiences in Birmingham and London respectively.

Source A

Lovers Rock, often dubbed 'romantic reggae' is a uniquely black British sound that developed in the late 70s and 80s against a backdrop of riots, racial tension and sound systems ... Lovers Rock allowed young people to experience intimacy and healing through dance--known as 'scrubbing'--at parties and clubs. This dance provided a coping mechanism for what was happening on the streets. Lovers Rock developed into a successful sound with national UK hits and was influential to British bands (Police, Culture Club, UB40).
(*The Story of Lovers Rock. Where to see?* From the *Black History Walks* website)

Source B

It has been three years since we lost two of the greatest singers in the Lover's Rock genre, namely Jean Adebambo and Louisa Marks. Both women made incredible contributions to the unique black British sound, which enjoyed its heyday in the UK during the 1970s and 80s ... Lover's Rock was dominated by women, whereas reggae on the whole before that era was dominated by men, and these women gave young girls the foresight to say we can be singers as well.
(Hazelann Williams, *The Queens of Lover's Rock,* in *The Voice,* 2 February 2013)

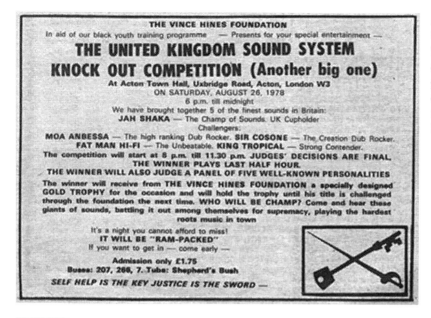

Advert for a Sound Clash in a West London Town Hall, 1978. The tradition of Sound Systems clashing with each other was still going strong in the Lovers Rock era. Moreover, Lovers Rock records were sold and promoted by the Sound Systems.

Source C

"We rejected the caution and restraint our parents had in a hostile racial environment," says poet Linton Kwesi Johnson. "We were the rebel generation – reggae afforded us our own identity." Singer Brinsley Forde, who helped found Aswad in 1975, echoes the sentiment. "What we sang about was our experience in London. People were copying Jamaica but weren't telling their own story." A key element of that story was police use of the hated "sus" laws, which allowed people to be picked up on "suspicion" of committing a crime, while hostility to the police was stoked by the deployment of phalanxes of cops to protect National Front marches through black areas.
(See Neil Spencer, *Reggae: the sound that revolutionised Britain,* in *The Guardian,* 30 January 2011)

ACTIVITIES . . .

1. Copy this out and fill in the gaps

_____ _____ was the first music created by Black British youngsters. They created a unique _____ sound that was not just a copy of _____ music. _____ artists dominated the production of Lovers Rock records. _____ _____ had a hit with when she was just 14. Janet Kay's hit single _____ _____ reached number 2 in the _____. Artists in Jamaica originally said this new music was _____. Outside of the Lovers Rock genre, Black Britons produced two superb Reggae bands: _____ and _____ _____.

Louisa Marks	romantic	Lover's Rock	Charts	fake
Jamaican	*Silly Games*	Women	Steel Pulse	Aswad

2. Read Source A. (i) What was meant by Lovers Rock providing a 'coping mechanism for what was happening on the streets'? (ii) Which bands did Lovers Rock influence?

3. Using Source B and other information, why do you think Lovers Rock was important to women?

4. From Source C, produce a list of all the reasons Reggae seemed important to young Black Britain.

Learning Objective: To show a fifth example of how Black culture influenced a Black and White youth subculture

The 2 Tone sound was started by young people, White and Black, from Coventry in the West Midlands. They grew up listening to 1960s music from Jamaica. The 2 Tone sound they created was mostly based on Ska (about 75%) mixed with Punk music (25%). The name '2 tone' came from a record label that was founded by White Coventry musician, Jerry Dammers, founder member of The Specials in the late 1970s. He was a central figure in the whole 2 Tone scene.

The bands associated with this genre were: The Specials, The Selector, The Beat, Body Snatchers, and Madness. They were all on the 2 Tone record label. *Gangsters* was The Specials' first two tone single, which went into the top ten of the charts. Bad Manners was another group with the 2 Tone sound but was not signed on their record label.

The logo for the record label was a Rude Boy: a man in a black suit, white shirt, narrow black tie, pork pie hat, white socks, and black loafers. Added to this was a black and white checked pattern, which was used to symbolise the 2 Tone genre. Wikipedia says the logo was loosely based on an early Ska album cover photo of Peter Tosh for his album *The Toughest*. Thus, the sharp and aspirational Rude Boy, Skinhead and Mod dress code influenced the 2 Tone fashion code.

Many of the early 2 Tone hits in the late 1970s were covers of original Jamaican Ska, Rocksteady, and Reggae records from the 1960s. Madness covered Prince Buster's *Madness*. They even took their name from this record. They also covered Buster's *One Step Beyond*. The Specials covered *A Message to you Rudy* originally by Dandy Livingstone. They also covered *Monkey Man*, originally performed by Toots and the Maytals.

The 2 Tone bands like The Specials and The Beat were mixtures of Black and White musicians. The Selector was largely Black, with Pauline Black as the lead singer – who was of Jewish and Nigerian heritage. Madness was all White. 2 Tone was the first youth subculture that was popular among the Asian community as well. Body Snatchers was an all-female group.

Even though 2 Tone was influenced by Black music and culture, Britain was still a racist place in the 2 Tone Years 1978-1983. It remains a fact that the success of the 2 Tone bands was negatively affected by how many Blacks were in the group. Madness, an all-White Skinhead group, had the most success, followed by Bad Manners, who were nearly all White. The groups with more Blacks in them had less success. Moreover, live performances of Madness and Bad Manners were marred by sieg-heiling Skinheads in their crowds.

Source A
Led by The Specials, a bunch of young groups lit up the charts with a potent home grown mix of British and Jamaican music. They brought with them a look that combined Black and White street styles. It wasn't just Britain's first multiracial music, it was a rich and contradictory movement born of turbulent times and the growing pains of multiculturalism.
(*2-Tone Britain*, Channel 4 television, 2004)

Source B
I moved around a lot as a kid, mainly around London, all over the place ... I always thought of Reggae and Ska and all that, as British music, I didn't really know where it was from. It was just part of the pop firmament.
(Graham "Suggs" McPherson, lead singer from Madness interviewed in *2-Tone Britain*, Channel 4 television, 2004)

Source C
It was a very inclusive movement, it felt like ... at the time. It was the sight of Black and White young men on stage performing music that harped back to a Black history, to Black musical tradition and combining it with quite political lyrics that reflected contemporary Britain and reflected the Thatcher's Britain that we were part of. That sense of no future, that sense of you're all on the scrap heap, if you're not part of the whole Tory movement of that time.
(Gurinder Chadha, an Asian 2 Tone head interviewed in *2-Tone Britain*, Channel 4 television, 2004)

ACTIVITIES . . .

1. What was 2 Tone? Who coined the name?

2. Name the bands that were associated with 2 Tone?

3. What is the evidence of CONTINUITY between the 2 Tone SOUND and 2 Tone FASHION with music and fashion from Jamaica? What is the evidence of CHANGE between the 2 Tone Sound and Jamaican music?

4. How did the 2 Tone scene bring people of different colours together?

5. In what way did racism impact on the success of the bands?

6. According to Source A, what was significant about 2 Tone?

7. Why would Suggs, lead singer of Madness (Source B), think that Ska and Reggae was British music?

8. Margaret Thatcher was the Prime Minister and the leader of the Conservative (or Tory) Party, the same organisation that produced Enoch Powell ten years earlier. Why did Gurinder Chadha (Source C) see 2 Tone as an inclusive scene that opposed what Margaret Thatcher stood for?

EXTENDED WRITING

Using your imagination, write the script of a telephone call between Gurinder Chadha and a friend. Gurinder had just realised that Asians could be an accepted part of the 2 Tone scene. How would the conversation go? What would she have felt?

Learning Objective: To show how Black Britain has continued to undergo demographic changes

Modern Black British culture was originally Trinidadian, and then Jamaican influenced. These cultures were brought here by Migrants. By the 1970s, a new Black British culture emerged amongst Blacks born in Britain. Added to this, new Black Migrants brought African cultures to Britain: Nigerian, Ghanaian and Somali. The Somalis entering Britain, largely in the 1990s, were the first group of Black Migrants allied to Islam rather than Christianity.

African Migrants came to Britain during the same Windrush period as the Caribbeans, but in lower numbers. However, an African character, Philip Smith, appeared in a British high-ranking comedy called *Rising Damp* which aired in 1974. Philip Smith (though acted by Trinidadian Don Warrington) was an African university student who was the son of a Chief. This was significant because there was a major social class difference between Africans and Caribbeans. Africans in Britain came from higher social class backgrounds.

In 1981 there were 699,000 Black people living in the UK of which 550,000 were Caribbeans and 123,000 were Africans. In 1991 this grew to 872,100 Black people of which 496,000 were Caribbeans but the African population increased to 203,200. This African growth is continuing.

Patti Boulaye was born in Nigeria in 1954. At the age of 16 she left Africa and came to London. She began her career as a West End stage actress with roles in the musical *Hair,* and *Two Gentlemen of Verona.* Boulaye was also a singer and dancer and was a member of an all-girl group. She recorded several singles. However, she made a massive impact on Black women by her colourful make-up, hair braids and extensions, and her fashion sense. Moreover, the English saw her as an exotic beauty. Many Black women in Britain gradually abandoned the 'roots and culture' look to copy her. This was the beginnings of more and more influence coming from Africa.

By the 1980s there was a boom in Africans on the music scene. Sade, of mixed English and Nigerian heritage, produced a massively commercial fusion of Jazz and Soul. Seal, of Nigerian heritage, created a highly distinctive Pop sound. MCs such as Skepta, his brother JME, and Tinie Tempah are popular on the Grime scene. However, these influences would not be the beginning of the British and African music interface. It is important to mention the earlier influence of Fela Kuti. His music represents the origins of Afrobeat.

Ghanaian musicians have also had a strong influence on Black British music, from traditional African music to Afrobeat, UK Garage, and Grime. Musicians such as Dizzee Rascal, Lethal Bizzle, Tinchy Stryder and Sway all became household names in the Grime scene and are of Ghanaian heritage. Currently, Stormzy is making a significant impact on the British Grime scene.

Source A

In the first couple of years, when I was a teenager, it was difficult to find a White agent who would take on a Black artist. I was told that I was lucky to get a job so I thought I might as well go this alone. But then Dick Katz, who was more of a friend than an agent, got me a job as a singer in a group and sorted out my Equity.

(Patti Boulaye, interview published on YouTube, 10 July 2010)

The Ambassador magazine, Summer 2010. The cover story highlights Tidjane Thiam, (from the Ivory Coast) the first Black CEO of a top British Company. It also names the Nigerian, Adebayo Ogunlesi, who now owns Gatwick Airport.

Source B

"At school, the African kids used to lie and say they were Jamaican." Those were the words of Skepta ... He spoke about how when the register was called he would try to say his Yoruba surname before his teacher had a chance to mangle it. It's a story thousands of British Nigerians can relate to and cringe at. He added: "So when I first came in the game and I'm saying lyrics like: 'I make Nigerians proud of their tribal scars / My bars make you push up your chest like bras', that was a big deal for me. All my early lyrics were about confidence. I can hear myself fighting back." For a new generation of British Nigerians that fight back feels complete.

(Lanre Bakare, *How Nigerian artists made their mark on British music,* in *The Guardian,* 9 August 2016)

ACTIVITIES . . .

1. In three steps, show how Black British culture evolved.

2. How did the Philip Smith character highlight the traditional social class difference between Africans who came to Britain and Caribbeans?

3. What was the significance of Patti Boulaye?

4. Of the musicians of Nigerian heritage mentioned, in your opinion, who was the most significant? Give a reason for your answer.

5. Of the musicians of Ghanaian heritage mentioned, in your opinion, who was the most significant? Give a reason for your answer.

6. According to Source A, what problems did Patti Boulaye face when trying to make it in showbiz?

7. According to Source B, how did Skepta bring pride to Blacks of Nigerian heritage living in Britain?

CLASS TWENTY-ONE: 1981: YEAR OF CONFRONTATION

Learning Objective: To learn about the most confrontational year in Black British history

Nineteen Eighty-One was a traumatic year for Black Britain, especially the youth. There were two defining events: The New Cross Massacre and the 1981 Riots.

On 18 January 1981, 13 young Blacks burned to death in a fire, during a party in New Cross. The Police and the Authorities claimed that the fire was an accident that started from inside the house. In the Black Community, however, nobody believed that. Blacks thought the fire was an arson attack that was racially motivated. Many thought the National Front were somehow involved.

The police investigation which concluded that the fire was accidental was criticised by Black activists including Darcus Howe. In response, Howe organised a march: Black Peoples Day of Action. The marchers walked the 17 miles from Deptford to Hyde Park to protest chanting: 'Thirteen dead and nothing said!' On route, they marched past the headquarters of *The Sun* newspaper where the journalists shouted racist abuse at the Black protesters from out of the windows.

Later that year, the police launched Swamp 81, a mass stop and search campaign against the Black youth. It resulted in 943 people being searched. Ten squads of police took part. Seventy-five people were charged with robbery. The police re-used an ancient vagrancy law to arrest Black people on 'sus' or 'suspicion'. This meant Black people could be arrested, tried, and jailed without ANY proof of committing a crime!

Four days after Swamp 81, there were major street battles between Black youth and the Metropolitan Police. Some call these battles 'riots', others call them 'uprisings.' The violence made international news. The conflicts started in Lambeth, South London. *Time* Magazine called this event 'Bloody Sunday.' Other violence swept the country in Black areas: Toxteth (Liverpool), Moss Side (Manchester), Handsworth (Birmingham), and Chapel Town (Leeds).

However, Margaret Thatcher's Conservative Party was in power in 1981. They were mostly unsympathetic to the Black youth. The media continued the demonization of Black youth that began in 1976. However, a few Conservative politicians saw the need to help the Black Community. The most important one was Lord Scarman. He set out a vision to help build a Black British middle class.

Source A
During the riot over 100 vehicles were burnt, 280 police injured, and 45 injuries to the public.
(*The Battle for Brixton*, BBC television, 2006).

Source B
[T]he uprisings of 1981 hung in the inner-city air, young Britons were absorbing the 'Don't push me, cause I'm close to the edge' message transmitted by Grandmaster Flash and the Furious Five ... to their own experience of ... unemployment, police harassment, drug abuse and racial disadvantage.
(Paul Gilroy, *There Ain't no Black in the Union Jack*, 1987, pp. 183-184)

A year before these Toxteth riots, there had been disturbances in St Paul's, Bristol, but 1981 brought riots to Brixton's streets in London and copy-cat rioting in Birmingham's Handsworth, Chappletown in Leeds, and Manchester's Moss Side.

(Lord David Alton, *The Riots of 2011 and the Riots of 1981,* from David Alton's website, 9 August 2011)

ACTIVITIES . . .

1. Copy this out and match the cause to the consequence

Cause	Consequence
Thirteen Blacks died in New Cross, so	Lord Scarman suggested ways forward
The Police said the fire was accidental, so	The police conducted an investigation
Police re-used an ancient 'sus' law, so	Darcus Howe led a Day of Action
Swamp 81 searched 943 Blacks, so	Huge numbers of Blacks were arrested
Black youth battled the police, so	Blacks came to resent the police
Some politicians wanted to help, so	The mass media demonized Black youth

2. Who did the Black Community think were responsible for the New Cross fire?

3. Why was the 'sus' law so unfair?

4. From Source A, what is the evidence that the police came out badly from the conflicts?

5. According to Source B, how did Grandmaster Flash's music speak for Black Britons?

6. Read Source C. Do you think that the conflicts outside London were merely copy-cat riots? Give a reason for your view.

EXTENDED WRITING

Use the Sources and other information to write a debate: *Uprisings or Riots?* Debates usually begin with the phrase: 'This House believes that ...' (i) Present evidence that would suggest that the battles were uprisings. You should start this section with the phrase: 'This House believes that the conflicts were uprisings.' (ii) Present evidence that would suggest that the battles were lawless riots. You should start this section with the phrase: 'This House believes that the conflicts were lawless riots.' (iii) Finally draw a conclusion to say whether you think the violence constituted uprisings or were merely lawless riots.

(The Teacher or Parent should decide if they think this task should be a spoken debate or a written task depending on the age and maturity of the pupils).

Lesson Objective: How did Black British History Month start?

After the 1981 conflicts, Black (and Asian) activists began entering local politics in large numbers. Encouraging Black and Brown people to vote for the Labour Party, these activists won control of many local councils across Britain. The first major success was in 1986. Merle Amory became the leader of Brent Council in North West London.

In power, the activists increased the numbers of Blacks and Asians in work. They encouraged Blacks and Asians to work in jobs connected to the local councils. Thus, for the first time in modern British history, Black and Brown people in large numbers worked in middle class council jobs. Consequently, Black workers did more than just the NHS, the Post Office, London Transport, British Rail and the factories. Moreover, the activists gave money to various community civil rights groups. This helped people feel they could make a difference to their own lives. They even sponsored music festivals that mixed music, culture, and politics.

However, these policies made enemies. Bigoted newspaper journalists inspired by the Conservative Party wrote articles that mocked these Labour policies. They called them: 'The Loony Left.'

Linda Bellos was a leading Labour activist who encouraged the mass employment of Black and Brown people by local councils. Of Jewish and Nigerian heritage, she was the Vice Chair of the Black sections campaign. They selected Africans, Caribbeans and Asians to become politicians within the Labour Party. She was also the second Black woman to become a leader of a British Local Authority in Brent, North West London. She was also a prominent figure that the newspapers mocked as 'Loony Left'. As head of the London Strategic Policy Unit, her team sponsored the first Black History Month in Britain in October 1987.

The Black History Month concept started as Negro History Week in America, 1926. Dr Carter G. Woodson started it and celebrated it in the month of February. The US government officially recognised Black History Month in 1976. In Britain, the Black History Month concept began with an activist of Ghanaian heritage, Akyaaba Addai Sebbo. He wanted to celebrate Africa's contribution to world civilisation. Supported by Ansel Wong, another activist, they suggested the idea to Linda Bellos who implemented it.

Source A

Most of the Windrush Generation who had arrived in the 50s and 60s worked in the Public Sector all their lives. Their children, if they found work at all, had gone the same route. But just months after the riots, a small group of Black and Asian activists in the North London Borough of Brent, opened a new approach to the problem. They set out to seize control of the largest single employer – the Local Council.
(*Windrush: A British Story*, Episode 4, BBC television, 1998)

Source B

Those who have no record of what their fore bears have accomplished lose inspiration which comes from the teaching of Biography and History.
(Carter G Woodson, M.S.N.B.C. 15 December 2005 Retrieved 14 February 2012)

Source C

I have been involved with Black History Month since early, 1987, when it started in the U.K. it was a political decision. The political term "black" meant African Caribbean and Asian origin, which was inclusive, to address racism ... Black History was about what we contributed to this country, people from the Commonwealth had a right to be here.
(Linda Bellos quoted in *The conversation: Why black history matters,* in *The Guardian,* 30 September 2011)

Source D

What has Africa contributed to the world? We have to bring it home ... So, we said we will organise activities to celebrate Africa's contribution to world civilisation from antiquity to the present.
(Akyaaba Addai Sebbo, interviewed in *History of British Black History Month,* on YouTube, 9 December 2012)

ACTIVITIES . . .

1. How did Black and Asian activists gain political power?

2. What difference did the new Labour councils make to the lives of Black and Brown people?

3. Why did the press come up with the term: 'The Loony Left'?

4. Give three facts about Linda Bellos.

5. (i) In four steps, explain how Black History Month started in the UK in 1987. (ii) Explain how Britain's Black History Month shows continuity with the United States in 1926. Explain also how it shows a change from 1926.

6. According to Source A, what was the main problem faced by Black youngsters in the early 1980s?

7. According to Source B (Carter G. Woodson), why is it important to study Black History?

EXTENDED WRITING

Write an essay called: *What should we teach in Black History Month?* Using Sources C and D, explain how Akyaaba Addai Sebbo's vision of Black History was very different to Linda Bellos' vision of Black History.

Learning Objective: To learn how Black Britons achieved mainstream sporting success

Randolph Turpin was the first great Black British boxer but his fame mostly predated the Windrush era. Of English and Guyanese heritage, some say he was Europe's best middleweight boxer of the 1940s and 1950s. There is a statue of him in Market Square, Warwick. Unlike Randolph Turpin, however, John Conteh became a household name in Black Britain. Of Irish and Sierra Leonean heritage, he competed from 1971 to 1980. On the advice of the legendary Muhammad Ali, Conteh fought at light-heavyweight level as opposed to heavyweight level. He won the WBC (World Boxing Council) light-heavyweight title in October 1974.

In the 1980s and 1990s, superb Black British boxers emerged: Lloyd Honeyghan, Nigel Benn, Chris Eubanks, Frank Bruno, and Lennox Lewis. They dominated the British game and became the first wave of Black British sporting success. Moreover, they were the first Black British sportsmen to achieve celebrity and wealth.

Lloyd Honeyghan, also known as Ragamuffin Man, competed from 1980 to 1995. He defeated American boxer Donald Curry in October 1986 to become the undisputed welterweight champion. Nobody expected him to win. He destroyed Curry in only six rounds. Honeyghan reigned twice as WBC, Ring magazine, and lineal welterweight champion between 1986 and 1989.

Nigel Benn, also called The Dark Destroyer, was a world champion in two weight divisions. He won the WBO (World Boxing Organisation) middleweight title in 1990, and held the WBC super-middleweight title from 1992 to 1996. BoxRec, a website of the sporting records of boxers, ranked Benn as the fourth best British super-middleweight boxer of all time.

Chris Eubanks won the WBO middleweight and super-middleweight titles. He scored victories over six world champions, one of whom was Nigel Benn in a gruelling 1990 fight. BoxRec ranked him as the third best British super-middleweight boxer of all time. He was a world champion for over five years and remained undefeated at middleweight level. His world title fights against Nigel Benn and Michael Watson helped British boxing ride a peak of popularity in the 1990s.

Frank Bruno won the WBC title in 1995 by defeating Oliver McCall at Wembley Stadium. He faced top-rated boxers during his career including two bouts with the legendary Mike Tyson and a domestic battle against Lennox Lewis. Bruno had excellent punching power: he won 38 of his 45 fights by knockout. He has remained popular with the British public following his retirement from boxing.

Lennox Lewis, also called The Lion, competed from 1989 to 2003. At 6 feet 5 inches tall, he was a three-time world heavyweight champion. He achieved the crown for the first time in December 1992 after Riddick Bowe gave up the title to avoid fighting him! In addition, he remains the last undisputed heavyweight champion. Many regard him as amongst the greatest heavyweight boxers of all time. In 1999, he was named Fighter of the Year by the Boxing Writers Association of America. He was also voted BBC Sports Personality of the Year.

Source A
I never even thought about the possibility of getting an honour – where I grew up the only letters you got were from the DHSS. It's an absolute privilege and an honour and I'm so grateful to all the people who supported me and put me forward for this award.
(John Conteh quoted in *John Conteh expresses gratitude over MBE award*, in *Daily Mail*, 16 June 2017)

Source B
The night of Sept 27, 1986, in Atlantic City, is etched into British boxing folklore. Twenty years ago today, Lloyd Honeyghan ripped, mauled and muscled the WBC, WBA [World Boxing Association] and IBF [International Boxing Federation] welterweights belts from a seemingly invincible Donald Curry. In boxing upsets, it ranks alongside Randolph Turpin's triumph over Sugar Ray Robinson in 1951.
(Gareth A. Davies, *Fight that shook the world*, in *The Telegraph*, 27 Sep 2006)

Source C
Here, Sportsmail takes a look at all seven Britons to have laid claim to the fabled 'richest prize in sport'.
BOB FITZSIMMONS (1897-99) ... MICHAEL BENTT (WBO, 1993-94) ... HERBIE HIDE (WBO, 1994-95 and 1997-99) ... FRANK BRUNO (WBC, 1995-96) ... HENRY AKINWANDE (WBO, 1996-97) ... LENNOX LEWIS (various 1993-94, 1997-2001, 2001-03) ... DAVID HAYE (WBA, 2009)
(*Bruno, Lewis, Haye and the rest of Britain's heavyweight champions of the world* in *Daily Mail*, 28 June 2011)

ACTIVITIES ...

1. Why was John Conteh a household name in Black Britain but Randolph Turpin was not?

2. (i) What did the Black boxers of the 1980s and 1990s achieve that was new for Black Britain? (ii) Explain why you think these achievements made them heroes in the Black Community.

3. Choose four of the boxers mentioned here and give three facts each about their achievements.

4. John Conteh in Source A mentions DHSS. This means Department of Health and Social Security and it refers to the government department that looks after poor, ill and unemployed people. With this in mind, what does Conteh mean by 'where I grew up the only letters you got were from the DHSS'?

5. According to Source B, what was significant about the boxing match on 27 September 1986?

6. Study Source C. Apart from Bob Fitzsimmons, everybody else listed is Black. How could this source be used to illustrate Black dominance over boxing from the 1990s?

7. Choose a fact with a date from the lives of the boxers mentioned here. Place the information on a time line from 1951 to 1999.

Learning Objective: To learn how Black Britons achieved mainstream sporting success

McDonald Bailey was the pioneering Black British Olympian. He competed at the 1948 and 1952 Olympics as a sprinter. He tied the world record of 10.2 seconds for 100 metres in 1951.

Tessa Sanderson was the first great Olympian to become a household name in the post Windrush era. She competed in all six Olympics from 1976 to 1996 as a javelin thrower. At the Commonwealth Games 1978, 1986 and 1990, she won gold medals. In the 1984 Summer Olympics in Los Angeles, she also won the gold medal. Like all the athletes mention here, she has received many honours and decorations. There is even a housing estate named after her in Wednesfield, West Midlands, called Sanderson Park.

Daley Thompson was a decathlete of Scottish and Nigerian heritage. In 1980, he broke the world decathlon record and won gold at the Moscow Olympics. In 1982, he set two new world records and won his second Commonwealth Games gold medal. In 1983, he won gold at the World Championships. He was thus the first athlete in the world to simultaneously hold gold in Olympic, World, continental and Commonwealth Games for a single event. In the 1984 Olympics, he won another gold and set a new world record. For all these achievements, many consider him to be one of the greatest decathletes of all time and the greatest all-round athlete Britain has ever produced.

Kriss Akabusi was a relay and hurdle athlete. As part of the British 4×400 metres relay team, he took gold medals at the 1986 Commonwealth Games and 1986 European Athletics Championships. He won the 1990 European Athletics Championships with a British record, and won gold at the 1990 Commonwealth Games. His 4×400 m relay team won at the World Championships in 1991. He followed this with a British 400 m hurdles record of 47.82 seconds to take the bronze medal at the 1992 Barcelona Olympics.

Linford Christie was a sprinter. He won gold at the 1992 Barcelona Olympics. He is the only man in Britain to have won gold for the 100 m at all four major competitions: the Olympics, the World Championships, the European Championships and the Commonwealth Games. The first man in Europe to break the 10 second barrier for the 100 m, he still holds the British record. He once held the world indoor record for the 200 m. He also held European records for the 60 m, 100 m and 4×100 m relay. With 24 major championship medals including 10 gold medals, he is the most decorated British male athlete.

Christine Ohuruogu is a 400 m sprinter and relay athlete. As a sprinter, she won gold at the 2008 Olympics in Beijing. She also won gold for the 400 m at the 2007 and 2013 World Championships. Moreover, she won six world championship medals in the women's 4 x 400 m relay as part of the Great Britain and Northern Ireland team.

Mo Farah is a distance runner. The most successful British track athlete in modern Olympic history, he won gold at the 2012 and 2016 Olympics in both the 5000 m and 10,000 m. He also completed the 'distance double' at the 2013 and 2015 World Championships. He is the first man in history to defend both distance titles in both major global competitions: Olympics and World. Since coming second in the 10,000 m at the 2011 World Championships, he has an unbroken winning streak: the 5000 m in 2011, and the double in 2012, 2013, 2015 and 2016. His achievements have been recognised. He became Sir Mo Farrah in 2013.

Source A
More than a third of Britain's London 2012 Olympic medal winners were born abroad or had a foreign parent or grandparent, a new study has suggested.
(*London 2012 Olympics: Third of Team GB medals 'won by immigrants'*, in *The Telegraph*, 14 Aug 2012)

Source B
The record-breaking achievements of Team GB athletes have reflected an inclusive and authentic pride in the shared, multi-ethnic society that we are today ... It's a different British Olympic team from the last London Games of 1948. Then, the popular sprinter McDonald Bailey from Trinidad stood out of the team photo as the only black athlete in a sea of white faces.
(Sunder Katwala quoted in *London 2012 Olympics: Third of Team GB medals 'won by immigrants'*, in *The Telegraph*, 14 Aug 2012)

ACTIVITIES . . .

1. Choose a fact with a date from the lives of the athletes mentioned here. Place the information on a time line from 1948 to 2013.

2. Why was Tessa Sanderson significant? List the ways that wider society has paid respect to her achievements.

3. Choose three of the athletes mentioned here and give four facts each about their achievements.

4. Using Sources A and B, suggest how Black Migrants, non-Black Migrants and their British born children and grandchildren have impacted on British athletics.

EXTENDED WRITING

Compose a piece of persuasive writing called *Black Britain's Best Athlete of All Times.* Choose one of the athletes and say why they are the most significant athlete in Black British History. You must support your answers with reasons.

Learning Objective: To learn how Black Britons achieved mainstream sporting success

British football has created more Black millionaires than any other area of work and industry. At one time, it was only a handful of Black musicians and boxers that enjoyed wealth. Football has surpassed both. The British game attracts, not just Black Britons, but Black talent from South America and Africa. Many became household names idolised by thousands of fans. However, it was not always so.

Clyde Best was a pioneer for Black footballers. He played at the top level in British football as part of the West Ham team between 1968 and 1976. He scored 47 goals for West Ham. However, racist fans regularly targeted him for abuse. Ultimately, he received an MBE from the Queen in 2006 for his services to football.

In 1978 West Bromwich Albion, a club in the old First Division, became the first team to field three black players: Cyrille Regis, Laurie Cunningham, and Brendon Batson. Since this was at a time of great racial tension, the three players were booed, subjected to monkey chants, and pelted with bananas by rival fans. Finding courage in their condemnation on and off the pitch, they were christened the 'Three Degrees'. (Incidentally, there was already an African American Soul group called The Three Degrees). The three footballers helped to break through the glass ceiling experienced by Black players. Becoming symbols of the social change sweeping the country, Brendon Batson went on to become the Deputy Chief Executive of the Player's Football Association.

In 1979 Viv Anderson became the first Black footballer to play for England. Two years later, Justin Fashanu became the first £1 million player in Britain. He achieved FA cup glory with Wimbledon in 1998 and scored 126 goals in his career. Other First Division Black players included Garth Crooks, Dave Bennet, and Gary Bennet.

In 1987 John Barnes became the first Black footballer to play for Liverpool, the most successful club in British football. As a player for England, he made 79 appearances. Barnes was Player of the Year twice, in 1987 and 1989. He recorded an official team song for England's 1990 World Cup: *World In Motion*. He was inducted into the English football Hall of Fame in 2005. He also managed Celtic and Jamaica. He is currently a football pundit for radio and television, a role he shares with Ian Wright.

Arsenal attracted a crop of Black players due partly to the fact that the club had much less racist abuse. Later legends at Arsenal included David Rocastle, Ian Wright, Sol Campbell, and Ashley Cole. They all went on to play for England. Wright became a television presenter and pundit. Cole, from 2001 to 2014, became a top performer as an England defender. He made 107 appearances.

Paul Ince broke through another glass ceiling for Black British players. He captained England in 1994 against Poland. He also broke through as a top-level football manager. He became the manager for Blackpool in 2013.

I enjoyed my footballing days [up to 1959]. Thought they were great. When I ran out ... they all went: 'Oooh! There's a Darkie playing!' ... but it wasn't said in any malice. It were just amazement because in them days, there weren't many Coloured footballers. Little did I realise that within twenty years it would be dominated by Coloured players.
(Charlie Williams, interviewed in *Windrush: A British Story,* Episode 4, BBC television, 1998)

Black footballers found themselves assailed by white hostility and hamstrung by white assumptions, 'No bottle, unreliable, don't like training, don't like the cold' ... All those ignorant views have got no foundation whatsoever.
(Dave Hill, *Out of his skin,* 1989, p. 94)

The three of us in one team, it was iconic, it was radical. We changed the face of football.
(Cyrille Regis quoted in *The Three Degrees* by Paul Rees, 2014, picture caption)

We thought that Laurie Cunningham and Cyrille Regis were gods. We saw them in that arena, scoring goals, doing something that no other black person that we knew of had ever done or achieved.
(Derrick Campbell quoted in *The Three Degrees* by Paul Rees, 2014, p. 64)

By 1995, the three most expensive players in Britain were Black. In the same year, Manchester United's Paul Ince captained England.
(*Windrush: A British Story,* Episode 4, BBC television, 1998)

ACTIVITIES . . .

1. Give your reasons why football has produced more Black millionaires than boxing or music.

2. Who were the Three Degrees? Why were they significant?

3. (i) List the achievements of each footballer: Viv Anderson, Justin Fashanu, Ashley Cole, John Barnes, and Paul Ince. (ii) Decide who you think has made the most important achievement and list them from 1 to 5. (iii) Give reasons for choosing your number one.

4. Copy out and complete this table.

Source	Information about Black footballers	Impression that wider society or other Blacks had about Black footballers
A		
B		
C		
D		
E		

Lesson Objective: How Black British Soul artists sold Soul back to the Americans and left a legacy

In the 1980s Black Britain created a British Soul scene. Due to the success of British artists in the United States, Americans called it the 'British Soul invasion'. Although heavily influenced by African American Soul, Black British Soul had a slightly different less Gospel influenced flavour. British Soul, like Lovers Rock, grew out of the life and experiences of the second generation Windrush era Blacks. However, the music and the imagery was more aspirational than Reggae from the same period. Black British Soul artists initially adopted a polished, suited, classy look. Their fans copied this aspirational attitude.

Junior's 1982 Soul anthem *Mama Used To Say* became a transatlantic hit. He became the first Black British singer to appear on America's legendary *Soul Train* television programme. The song earned him Billboards 'Best Newcomer Award', presented by the Godfather of Soul musicians: James Brown. He won a Grammy for his song *Do You Really Want My Love*, which featured on *The Beverley Hills Cop* film soundtrack in 1984. Other classics were *Oh Louise, Morning Will Come* and *Too Late*. A pioneer in his field, Junior was the first artist to present British based Black music to audiences outside of the UK.

Sade was a Soul artist of English and Nigerian heritage. She became a huge sensation in America with her 1984 song *Smooth Operator*. Combining Soul with Jazz, she made a cameo appearance in the film *Absolute Beginners*. Sade became, in fact, one of the most successful British artists of all time. All her albums went Platinum in America.

Loose Ends achieved their first success hit with *Hangin' on a String* in 1985, which reached number 13 in the UK chart and number 1 in the US Billboard R & B chart. Other significant Black British Soul artists in the 80s and 90s were Mica Paris, Andrew Roachford, Mark Morrison, Omar, Jaki Graham, Rick Clarke, Don-E, Beverley Knight and Lynden David Hall.

Soul II Soul were a British Soul collective who flourished in London from 1987 to 1997. Their UK number 1 *Back To Life (However Do You Want Me)* became a Top 5 hit in the United States. *Keep On Moving* was another transatlantic success. Soul II Soul initially attracted attention as a sound system, playing records at house parties. Founded by Jazzie B and later joined on lead vocals by Caron Wheeler, their fashion sense spurned a new style dubbed 'Funki Dred' (i.e. Funky Dreads). They also created a line of clothing by that name. Those who imitated this style typically wore their hair in 'locs', sometimes just at the top of the head and shaved around the sides. This 'funki dred' phenomenon reached America and influenced the youth culture there. Before this period, African Americans did NOT wear 'locs'. Soul II Soul's album: *Club Classics Volume One,* peaked at number 1 on the UK Albums chart in 1989 and sold over 4 million copies worldwide.

Source A
American soul music has a direct link to its African roots, whereas British soul, in its original form, came with a heavy dose of Caribbean influence ... Towards the end of the disco era, young British soul musicians were well entrenched and felt the need to find their own voice.
(Angus Batey, *UK soul: the sound of the Union,* in *The Guardian,* 7 July 2011)

The Funki Dred was a combination of lots of different religious and spiritual ideas and energies ... Many of us went to church but there was a lot of rebelliousness going on in terms of people trying to find out about their identity ... We'd just gone through the whole afro-centric thing in America where people again wanting to find out about their roots and naturally, as soundmen we were heavily involved in reggae and Dub music. All these different ideas were rubbing off and we just really wanted to bring a sense of our own identity, so instead of just having our own long dreadlocks, we decided to come up with a style ... We borrowed a little bit of this spirituality and that philosophy and so on and came up with what we called The Funki Dred and lo and behold, it took on a life of its own and took off. I think a lot of people were able to identify with it – black, white, yellow, pink and brown, bringing forth all these different ideas and marrying it with both music and fashion with our own style, flipping the script a little bit.

(Soul II Soul: The day of the Funki Dred, from the B & S [i.e. Blues and Soul] website, issue 1081)

ACTIVITIES . . .

1. Why do Americans speak of the 'British Soul invasion'?

2. What was different about the image projected by the Soul artists (compared to the Reggae artists)?

3. In what three ways was Junior a pioneer?

4. What is the evidence that Sade was a success?

5. What was significant about Loose End's *Hangin' on a String*?

6. What were the range of cultural products Soul II Soul brought to the market place? What legacy did they leave in America?

7. According to Source A, what is the difference that heritage made on British Soul compared to American Soul?

8. According to Source B, what did the 'Funki Dreds' symbolise?

EXTENDED WRITING

Write a proposal (called a 'sales pitch') for the management at the African American television programme, *Soul Train*. You should suggest why Soul II Soul should be booked on to the show. Mention why their new look would be a sensation in the United States. Mention how Black British musicians have been successful in the United States in the past (e.g. Junior, Sade, and Loose Ends).

Learning Objective: What was the second musical culture Black Britons invented in the UK?

Jungle had its origins in Hackney, East London, around 1989. Black British DJs like Terry T and Grooverider experimented with fusing Reggae, Soul and Techno with break beats using similar techniques to those used by HipHop DJs. Old records were 'sampled' and mixed into fast frenetic dance beats with heavy Ragga baselines. Most of the early Jungle tracks were produced by young people in their bedrooms on computer systems. Its 'golden years' were 1994 and 1995 when some songs became top 40 hits.

Jungle was mostly influenced by Ragga baselines and Jamaican vocals. The formula of having a turntable, a DJ and an MC is coming directly from the roots of Jamaican sound systems. Jungle DJs would have sound clashes with Jungle tunes, similar to sound systems clashing with Reggae and Dancehall songs. Jungle music remained underground and was played mainly in clubs and pirate radio stations. Jungle clubbers adopted the tough, ghetto, streetwise look of Jamaican Dancehall Reggae.

By 1994, Jungle received bad press with it being associated with Black youth crime and gangster culture. For the first time in recent history, Black youth gangs targeted each other for violence. Consequently, some suggested that Jungle should have a new name. Eventually, 'Drum & Bass' was agreed upon by Goldie and the other top producers. The music did evolve over this period, however. Jungle era music had more vocals; but Drum and Bass became more instrumental with a simpler production.

Jungle records such as *Sweet Love, The Burial, Helicopter, Lighter,* and *Super Sharp Shooter* are just a few of the Jungle songs that were popular amongst the youth. General Levy's *Incredible,* produced by M. Beat was the first Jungle song to appear on Top of the Pops in 1994. Jungle also appealed to the young Asian community, similar to the appeal of 2 Tone music. Evidence of this is the collaboration by Shy FX and UK Apachi with *Original Nuttah,* which also made it into the pop charts. Congo Natty's *Junglist* was another cross over record in 1995.

Source A
If you take the emergence of computer technology, particularly the Atari, around 1990 onwards, it provided an opportunity for a lot of urban youngsters, black and white, to actually inform the music with their own sampling, with their own experiences, and to make the music a bit more relevant to what they wanted to hear and what they were feeling. The computer technology just created a whole generation of bedroom Junglists.
(Koushik Banerjea, Lecturer Goldsmith College, interviewed in *All Black: Jungle Fever,* BBC television, 1994)

Source B
Jungle has been called the sound of urban Britain. It takes dance music back to its black roots. It emerged in the late 80s as a break-away from the rave scene when DJs started experimenting with black sounds. Until then rave music attracted a largely white audience but Jungle's rhythms and baselines appealed to black youth. In the last year, Jungle has grown from a small exclusive underground scene to the main sound on the streets. Over the summer 20,000 were raving to Jungle every weekend. In London, major west end clubs now feature Jungle. Even radio 1 has begun to play it.
(*All Black: Jungle Fever,* BBC television, 1994)

There is a new generation of people who have grown up to rave culture to whom that was their punk music, who do hear music in a different way, who've grown up through hearing music in clubs, loud, dancing, going to raves, driving around the M25, looking for search lights in the sky, that is their Friday and Saturday night. So I do think for a real appreciation of what's going on, you have to get into that frame of mind. You've got to stop saying it doesn't sound like the Beatles. It just sounds different.
(Ben Watt, musician interviewed in *Roni Size: The Works Documentary*, BBC television, 1997)

Source D

I'm half Arab, half Asian-African, I can relate to those countries only up to a point. When I talk to my children, I can't talk to them about Africa, I can't talk to them about where my dad's from, because my life has not been there, my life has been in England and London. I have to talk to them about Balham, Tooting, where I'm from. So, if you're born in England, be proud of it. And don't make nobody tell you no different, no BNP [i.e. British National Party], or anything like that. The Jungle is British, I can really relate to it and it's our music.
(UK Apachi, interviewed in *All Black: Jungle Fever*, BBC television, 1994)

ACTIVITIES . . .

1. What was Jungle? Who started it?

2. In what ways was Jungle similar to Reggae Sound Systems? In what ways was Jungle different from Reggae Sound Systems?

3. What was the media perception of Jungle? How did Black youth culture change during this period? Why is this a problem?

4. Name the three Jungle tunes that achieved commercial success.

5. According to Source A, how did new technology democratise the making of music? Why is this a revolutionary change?

6. Using Source B, explain in four steps how Jungle became popular.

7. According to Source C, why might youngsters who grew up after the Rave Era hear music differently to youngsters of the Beatles' time?

8. According to UK Apachi (Source D), how can Jungle bring people of different colours together? In what way does this show continuity with earlier musical forms such as 2 Tone (Class 19)?

Lesson Objective: To learn how Black Britons achieved mainstream success

Andrew Salkey came from Panama to Britain in the 1950s to pursue a university education. A prolific writer and editor, he was the author of more than 30 books over his career. He wrote novels for adults, novels for children, poetry collections, anthologies, travelogues and essays. His importance has been recognised. Hampshire College has an award for students who show exceptional writing promise called The Andrew Salkey Memorial Scholarship.

E. R. Braithwaite wrote *To Sir, With Love* (1959) based on his experiences as a school teacher in East London. It won an Anisfield-Wolf Book Award. *To Sir, with Love* was adapted into a film, starring Sidney Poitier.

Linton Kwesi Johnson is a poet, journalist, and author. He wrote poems influenced by racial turbulences of the 1960s and 1970s. He is the leading exponent of Dub Poetry, with lyrics delivered over heavy reggae bass lines.

John Agard is a playwright, author, and poet. He published two books while in Guyana before moving to England in 1977. Although brought up in an English colonial education, he wrote in Guyanese Creole and used a Caribbean style of speaking when performing his poems. Grace Nichols, his wife, is also a poet. They won many awards for their contribution to poetry. Both contributed to the classic 1994 school text, *A Caribbean Dozen*.

Benjamin Zephaniah was one of *The Times* 2008 list of Britain's top 50 post-war writers. His first book of poetry, *Pen Rhythm,* aimed to fight the dead image of poetry in academia, and to 'take [it] everywhere' to people who do not read books. His second collection *The Dread Affair: Collected Poems* (1985), contained poems attacking the British legal system. *Rasta Time in Palestine* (1990) was an account of a visit to the Palestinian occupied territories. Zephaniah was poet in residence at the chambers of Michael Mansfield QC.

Andrea Levy is an award-winning author of five novels. Her fourth novel, *Small Island,* won the 2004 Orange Prize for Fiction, the 2004 Whitbread Book of the year, and the 2005 Commonwealth Writers Prize. It was also adapted for BBC television and broadcast in 2009.

Malorie Blackman wrote *Not So Stupid!* a book of short stories. She wrote scripts for television, including several episodes for *Whizziwig, Byker Grove,* and *Pig-heart Boy.* Her most well-known books are the school classics: *Noughts & Crosses, Knife Edge,* and *Checkmate.* She won the Nestle Smarties Book prize (Silver award); twice won Wirral Children's Book award (1999 and 2003). From 2013 to 2015, she was the Waterstone's Children's Laureate.

Zadie Smith is the author of five novels: *White Teeth, The Autograph Man,* and *Swing Time.* Her novel, *On Beauty,* won the 2006 Orange Prize for fiction. An excerpt from another novel, *NW,* won a 2014 ASME National Magazine award for fiction. Moreover, she won the Guardian First Book Award in 2000, the WH Smith Award for Best New Talent, 2001, the Sunday Times Young Writer of the Year Award, 2003, and the British Book Awards Decibel Writer of the year, 2006. Channel 4 Television adapted *White Teeth* in 2002 as a four-part series.

Source A

[T]he work coming from what has often been called "the margins"--from the immigrants, their children and their children's children--is invigorating British writing with a new vitality ... There is Linton Kwesi Johnson, widely regarded as the father of dub poetry; Malorie Blackman, the highly successful children's author whose novel Noughts and Crosses *was one of the books on the BBC's The Big Read Top 100 list; Ben Okri, who won the Booker Prize for his novel* The Famished Road.
(Andrea Levy, *Made in Britain,* in *The Guardian,* 18 September 2004)

Source B

[M]y motivation sprang from a visceral need to creatively articulate the experiences of the black youth of my generation, coming of age in a racist society.
(Linton Kwesi Johnson, *The Guardian,* 28 March 2012)

Source C

My father brought back from England an extraordinary collection of books. He came to London (from Nigeria) to train as a lawyer ... but he got carried away with being a successful young lawyer and didn't get round to reading them. They gathered dust and every now and then he'd say to me, "Ben, dust the books – but don't read them!" That made the books fantastically attractive ... I'd read for hours until I'd hear his voice ... and then I'd start dusting again.
(Ben Okri, interview for *The Guardian,* by Juliet Rix, 26 June 2010)

Source D

I wrote straight pastiche: Agatha Christie stories, Wodehouse vignettes, Plath poems – all signed by their putative authors and kept in a drawer. I spent my last free summer before college reading, among other things, Journal of the Plague Year, Middlemarch, and the Old Testament. By the time I arrived at college I had been in no countries, had no jobs, participated in no political groups, had no lovers ... In short, I was perfectly equipped to write the kind of fiction I did write: saturated by other books.
(Zadie Smith, interview for *The Guardian* by Aida Edemarium, 3 September 2005)

ACTIVITIES . . .

1. Why were Andrew Salkey and E. R. Braithwaite significant?

2. Choose four of the authors mentioned here and give three facts each about their achievements.

3. What point is Source A making?

EXTENDED WRITING

Using Sources B, C, and D, suggest how different situations motivate different people to create literature and achieve success. Finally, say what you think is an effective way to get inspiration to write.

Lesson Objective: To learn how Black Britons achieved mainstream success
With an acting career going back 50 years, Rudolf Walker starred in *Love Thy Neighbour,* becoming the first Black character to appear in a major British TV series. He has appeared in *EastEnders* for many years, taking on the role of Patrick Trueman. He also appeared in the American version of *Teletubbies*, where he narrated the opening and closing sequences.

Norman Beaton was known to millions from the Channel 4 television series *Desmond's*. He performed opposite Denzel Washington in *The Mighty Quinn* (1989), as well as an appearance in the hugely popular *The Cosby Show*. At its peak, *Desmond's* attracted 5.6 million viewers every week. It is still the most successful comedy series produced for Channel 4.

Carmen Munroe is known for her role as Shirley in *Desmond's*. She made her debut in 1962 at the Wyndham Theatre in London in *Period Adjustment.* She went on to perform leading roles in other West End productions. She performed in Lorraine Hansberry's *A Raisin in the Sun*, Alice Childress's *Trouble in Mind* and James Baldwin's *The Amen Corner*. She had high-profile roles in the late 1970s TV sitcoms *The Fosters* and *Mixed Blessings*. In 1986, she co-founded the Talawa Theatre Company – a pioneering Black British theatre company.

Adrian Lester trained at the Royal Academy of Dramatic Arts (RADA) in London. He played Mickey Bricks in the BBC television series *Hustle* between 2004 and 2012. He was awarded the Laurence Olivier award in 1996 for Best Actor in a Musical. On American television, Lester played the character Ellis Carter in the successful sitcom *Girlfriends*.

Chiwetel Ejiofor played the Shakespearean role of Othello as a teenager. Reclaiming that role in 2007 at the Donmar Warehouse, a critic at The Guardian described him as "the best Othello for generations." At 19 he landed a part in the 1997 film *Amistad.* Other roles followed in *Dirty Pretty Things*, *Serenity*, *Kinky Boots*, *Talk to Me* and *Redbelt*. He was nominated for three Golden Globes and nominated for an Academy Award for his role in the 2013 masterpiece *12 Years a Slave*. Ejiofor has worked with Spike Lee, appeared with Denzel Washington in *American Gangster,* starred alongside Angelina Jolie in *Salt,* and starred in *Half of a Yellow Sun*. He played the great Congolese politician, Patrice Lumumba, in the *Season of the Congo* in 2013.

Sophie Okonedo, of Jewish and Nigerian heritage, studied at RADA. She was nominated in 2004 for an Academy Award as best supporting actress in *Hotel Rwanda.* She won a Tony award in 2014 for the Broadway production *A Raisin in the Sun*, which also starred Denzel Washington. She worked alongside Adrian Lester in BBC One's six-part thriller, *Undercover.* She was nominated for a BAFTA for her lead role in a 2010 biopic of Winnie Mandela.

Idris Elba achieved fame playing Stringer Bell in the American crime series *The Wire*. He starred in the BBC detective drama *Luther*, for which he won a Golden Globe in 2012. Not originally written for a Black actor, Elba auditioned for the role of DCI John Luther and won the role. Elba also starred in *Mandela: Long Walk to Freedom,* for which he received a Golden Globe nomination. More recently, he starred in the thriller *No Good Deed,* and the Netflix drama *Beasts of No Nation*.

Photograph from *Calypso,* a 1948 West End play with an all-Black cast. Edric Connor, the first great Windrush era actor, starred in the performance.

Source A

The star says a lack of big roles for black and Asian talent in British TV is forcing non-white performers to the US where they can land better parts
(*Lenny Henry: Black actors quitting UK for US because of a lack of work,* in *The Mirror,* 15 December 2013)

Source B

There's a black British Actor Renaissance of sorts occurring, largely because black Brits aren't finding the type of work in the United Kingdom that allows them to explore the depth they're seeking from their roles. But stateside, these British expatriates are giving life to classic American stories, many gritty and all of them deeply layered and complex.
(Kelly L. Carter, *The Rise Of The Black British Actor In America,* on BUZZFEED NEWS website, 5 January 2015)

Source C

There are a lot of black British actors in these movies ... They're cheaper than us, for one thing. They don't cost as much. And they [casting agents and directors] think they're better trained, because they're classically trained.
Samuel L. Jackson quoted in *Samuel L Jackson criticises casting of black British actors in American films,* in The Guardian, 8 March 2017)

ACTIVITIES . . .

1. Why was Rudolf Walker significant?

2. Choose three of the actors mentioned here and give four facts each about their achievements.

3. Using Sources A, B, and C, suggest how Black actors have impacted on Britain and on America.

Lesson Objective: To learn how Black Britons achieved mainstream success

Ronald Moody was a pioneering Black artist. Of Jamaican heritage, he came to Britain to study dentistry in 1923. Inspired by Ancient Egyptian art, he became a sculptor working in wood. Best known for his great female head, *Midonz* in 1937, exhibitions of his work were held in Paris and Amsterdam. He settled in the UK in 1941 where his work was regularly exhibited throughout the 1950s and 1960s. His art featured in the remarkable 2015 exhibition *No Colour Bar: Black British Art in Action 1960-1990*.

George Kelly was another sculptor of Jamaican heritage featured in the *No Colour Bar* exhibition. He exhibits under the Yoruba name 'Fowokan'. Largely self-taught, he has practised sculpture since 1980, following a trip to Nigeria. His bust of Mary Seacole is particularly notable.

Christopher Ofili is a painter of Nigerian heritage. He won the Turner Prize in 1998, the most important yearly award in British fine art. He studied cave paintings in Zimbabwe and his work shows the influence of the brilliant African American artist Jean-Michel Basquiat. His paintings *The Holy Virgin Mary* of the Black Madonna, and *No Woman No Cry* dedicated to Lady Doreen Lawrence, are particularly important. He received a CBE for services to art.

Steve McQueen, a video artist, won the Turner Prize in 1999. His film, *12 Years a Slave,* won an Academy Award, BAFTA Award for Best Film, and Golden Globe Award for Best Motion Picture. He also won Best Director from the New York Film Critics Circle. For services to the visual arts, he received a CBE. *Time* magazine in April 2014 listed him as amongst the 100 most influential people in the world. In 2016, he obtained the British Film Institute's highest honour, the BFI Fellowship.

Yinka Shonibare produces figures decorated by bright Dutch wax textiles worn in African countries. His 2002 *Gallantry and Criminal Conversation*, made of mannequins and a suspended carriage, won international acclaim. He was awarded an MBE in 2004 for his services to art. He was elected Royal Academician by the Royal Academy of Arts in 2013. His work explores cultural and racial identity in a globalised world.

Continuing the theme of textiles, Black Britain has produced some of Britain's leading tailors of our time and an internationally acclaimed catwalk queen.

Andrew Ramroop began work as a Savile Row tailor in 1970. Savile Row in Central London has been the centre of high quality gentlemen's clothing since the Eighteenth Century. Ramroop was at one time the President of the Master Tailors Association. Following this in 2008, he started The Savile Row Academy that trains new generations of tailors to maintain classic standards. He has dressed Samuel L. Jackson and Princess Diana.

Ozwald Boateng has the highest public profile of all the Savile Row tailors. He has dressed Hollywood stars and has made Savile Row clothing popular with younger people. In 2006, an eight-part documentary was screened in the US called *House of Boateng*.

Naomi Campbell is a Queen of the Catwalk. Recruited at the age of 15, she established herself among the top three most recognisable and in-demand models in the world of the late 1980s and the 1990s. She was one of six models of her generation to be declared 'supermodels' by the fashion industry.

Source A

My work is rooted in the traditions of pre-colonial Africa and ancient Egypt rather than the Greco Roman art of the west. Coming to the visual arts late in life I deliberately chose not to be trained in western art institutions as I felt that these institutions could not teach me what I wanted to know. They were too deeply entrenched in their own traditions with little or no understanding or interest in the things that interested me most, which are the ideas that lie behind the art and culture of Africa.
(George Kelly, *About* from the website *Fowokan: One who creates with the hand*)

Source B

In 1988 Maurice Sedwell was purchased from the retiring Maurice Sedwell by Andrew Ramroop, a long-standing employee. The business thrived in the 1980s and 1990s with a client list littered with Lords, Politicians, and even a member of the royal family. In 1994 the business moved to the larger premises of 19 Savile Row.
(*Maurice Sedwell*, from Wikipedia)

Source C

In August 1988, she became the first black model to appear on the cover of French Vogue, after her friend and mentor, designer Yves St. Laurent, threatened to withdraw his advertising from the magazine if it continued to refuse to place black models on its cover. The following year, she appeared on the cover of American Vogue, which marked the first time a black model graced the front of the September magazine, traditionally the year's biggest and most important issue.
(*FAB Fashion: Top 30 Naomi Campbell Vogue Covers*, from the website *Fab Magazine Online*, 31 October 2013)

ACTIVITIES . . .

1. What is the evidence that Christopher Ofili and Steve McQueen reached the top of the game?

2. Choose four of the individuals mentioned here and give three facts each about their achievements.

3. According to George Kelly, Source A, why is it difficult for a Black artist to study the African art tradition in the UK?

4. What is the evidence presented in Sources B and C that show that Andrew Ramroop and Naomi Campbell were at the top of the game?

EXTENDED WRITING

Dr David Starkey (Class 1) claimed that the Black contribution to Britain was "a particular sort of violent, destructive, nihilistic, gangster culture." Using the information presented here, say whether you think he is right or wrong and support your answer with evidence.

Lesson Objective: To learn how Black Britons achieved mainstream political influence

After SS Empire Windrush in 1948, it took many years for Black people to enter mainstream political positions. In 2011 there were 1,904,684 Black people living in the UK, 3 percent of the population, of which over 989,628 were Africans and over 594,825 were Caribbeans.

Learie Constantine became the first Black member of the House of Lords in 1969. Originally a cricketer, lawyer, and Trinidad's High Commissioner to the United Kingdom, he became Baron Constantine of Maraval and Nelson. After him, David Pitt, a Labour Party politician of Grenadian heritage and medical doctor, became the second Black member of the House of Lords in 1975. He became Baron Pitt of Hampstead.

The General Elections in 1987 was historic because it was the first time that 3 Black British people were elected as Members of Parliament (MPs): Bernie Grant, Paul Boateng, and Diane Abbott. Paul Boateng of Scottish and Ghanaian heritage became the first Black member of the Cabinet. Since then, there have been many more Black and Mixed Heritage MPs. As with the Lords, most were Labour Party members but a few were Conservatives.

Valerie Amos was a Labour Party politician of Guyanese heritage. She became a member of the House of Lords in 1997 becoming Baroness Amos of Brondesbury. When she became Secretary of State for International Development in 2003, she also became the first Black woman member of the Cabinet. Later that year, she became Leader of the House of Lords. Finally, in 2015, she became Director of The School of Oriental and African Studies (SOAS), becoming the first Black woman to lead a British university.

Dr John Sentamu was an Anglican church minister of Ugandan heritage. He served as the Bishop of Stepney and later the Bishop of Birmingham. In 2005, he became the 97th Archbishop of Canterbury, the second most powerful position in the English Church. He is a member of the Privy Council and a member of the House of Lords. In 2008, the Archbishop Thurstan Church of England School, Hull, was renamed in his honour. It is now the Archbishop Sentamu Academy.

Bill Morris was a trade unionist of Jamaican heritage. Trade unionists represented the interests of workers. In 1991, he became General Secretary of the Transport & General Union. In 2000, he was elected to the head of the Trades Union Congress. This made him the most powerful trade union leader in the United Kingdom. It also made him the most powerful Black man in the country. He became a member of the House of Lords in 2006 becoming Baron Morris of Handsworth.

Patricia Scotland was a lawyer of Dominican heritage. She became a member of the House of Lords in 1997 becoming Baroness Scotland of Asthal. On 28 June 2007, she became Attorney General, the most powerful lawyer in the country. She was the first AND ONLY woman to hold the office in 700 years. As Attorney General, she was the chief legal adviser to the Queen, to Parliament, and to the Government.

Source A
Now dat wi got wi MP, and wi Black JP.
Blacks 'pon de radio, Blacks 'pon TV.
Wi Sir, and wi Lord, and wi MBE.
But ah it dat?
(Linton Kwesi Johnson quoted in *Counterblast: Independant Intavenshan*, BBC television, 1999)

Source B
We meet on the eve of Bill Morris's election to the TUC presidency, the final rung on an extraordinary career ladder, which began when he arrived in Birmingham from Jamaica at the age of 16 ... He got a job in an engineering company, joining the Transport and General Workers' Union (TGWU) four years later. Becoming a shop steward, he rose through the ranks to become Britain's first black trade union leader. For the past nine years, he has been general secretary of the TGWU.
(Helena de Bertodano, *The inner pain of Bill Morris,* in *The Telegraph,* 10 September 2000)

Source C
She went down in the history books in 1999 as the first black woman to serve as a Government minister. Then ... in June 2007, she added a double distinction ... becoming both the first black Attorney General and the only woman to hold the post.
(*Attorney General Baroness Scotland: Lady Scotland was seen as a safe pair of hands,* in *The Telegraph,* 22 September 2009)

ACTIVITIES . . .

1. (i) Draw a time line from 1948 to 2010 of 8 facts from these 2 pages. (ii) Using your time line, who officially represented Black Britons from 1948 to 1968? (iii) Why might this have been a problem?

2. Why was 1987 considered 'historic'? How does this represent major cultural change?

3. Read paragraph 3 (on Lady Amos). What do you think is her most important achievement? Give a reason for your answer.

4. Compared to the other Lords and Ladies, what was different about Dr John Sentamu?

5. Why was Lord Morris once considered 'the most powerful Black man' in Britain?

6. Lord Morris was born in 1938. He became a shop steward (i.e. worker's representative) in 1962. Use Source B to draw up a time line on his achievements from 1954 to 2006.

7. In your opinion, using Source C on Lady Scotland, what is the most impressive achievement? becoming the first BLACK Attorney General or the first WOMAN Attorney General? Give a reason for your answer.

Learning Objective: What was the third musical culture Black Britons invented in the UK?

Emerging from Jungle, and influenced by African American HipHop and Garage music, Black British musicians pioneered UK Garage. This genre has since evolved into Grime. DJ Wookie created the UK Garage beat. The evolution continued with the So Solid Crew from Battersea, London, who achieved mainstream success in early 2001. This 35 strong UK Garage unit paved the way for the current generation of Grime stars to crossover and gain chart recognition.

White fans of UK Garage and Grime borrowed Black culture for a sixth time. They copied the sportswear, designer labels, hoop earrings and bling appearance. They became the Chavs (see Class 1). The cultural influences, however, went both ways. Black youngsters influenced by the Chavs started getting tattoos for the first time.

So Solid Crew released *Oh No* as their debut single in 2001. This was the first UK Garage recording of consequence. Performing as a 35-strong unit or as smaller combinations of DJs and MCs, the So Solid family included MC Harvey, Swiss, Oxide & Neutrino, Lisa Maffia, Romeo, Asher D and Megaman, its leader and visionary. Even Mystique, a more commercial group, were affiliated to the Crew. Perhaps the finest MC to emerge from the scene was Ms Dynamite. Known for her ability to rhyme in a Jamaican style with complex rhythmic and lyrical patterns, she occasionally performed with So Solid Crew.

Wiley, regarded as the Godfather of Grime, created a new sound from the East London housing estates in Bow. In the early 2000s, Wiley released a series of highly influential eskibeat instrumentals on white label vinyl. He also found fame as the pioneering Grime MC. He gathered a group of artists around him, the Roll Deep crew.

Grime grew in popularity within the underground music scene via pirate radio stations, independent records, clubs and sound clashes (two MCs battling with their lyrics). The Roll Deep crew became the training ground for Dizzee Rascal, Tinchy Stryder, and Skepta. These artists took Grime mainstream, achieving commercial success. Tinchy Strider even topped the UK pop charts on two occasions. Other successes were Kano and Wretch 32. Finally, in 2003 Channel U television emerged to champion UK Garage and Grime. It is also known as Channel AKA.

Source A

So Solid Crew are the UK hip-hop collective that brought grime and underground garage to the masses. Their 2001 single '21 Seconds' was a blockbuster hit, gaining the group their one and only Number One single in the UK, and bagging the group a BRIT award as well as recognition across the world.
(Alim Kheraj, *So Solid Crew then and now: what happened to Romeo, Lisa Maffia, MC Harvey and the rest?* from the *Digital Spy* website, 12 April 2016)

Source B

Wiley's new sound owed something to its glitzier chart-friendly predecessor, UK garage, but it was darker, stranger, and harder to dance to. As UK garage's star waned, other pioneering young artists joined Wiley on the dark side, and this new sound quickly evolved on the thriving pirate radio stations of inner London. The genre was defined by local "crews" of friends, usually containing a DJ or two, a few producers, and a host of MCs passing the mic. In 2003, the world beyond the range of the pirate

stations' transmitters started to catch on. That summer, Wiley's protege Dizzee Rascal released his debut album Boy in da Corner, *which went on to win the Mercury prize and drew attention to this new scene.*
(Dan Hancox, *Wiley: The enigmatic Godfather of Grime,* in *The Guardian,* 24 January 2017)

Source C
By early 2003, the underground buzz around grime was intensifying and the crews had better radio transmitters, capable of reaching out to new parts of east London ... Channel U, a new music TV station launched in February 2003, provided a visual platform for the scene, featuring cheaply produced videos, usually shot on handheld cameras. By that summer, the crackling energy coming out of the pirates grew louder, peaking with the arrival of Dizzee Rascal's album Boy in da Corner. *When it won the Mercury that autumn, A&R men descended on east London.*
(Dan Hancox, *Wiley: The enigmatic Godfather of Grime,* in *The Guardian,* 24 January 2017)

Source D
Channel U was radical at a time when black British artists weren't being readily supported on mainstream channels, radio or labels. Launched in 2003, Channel U epitomised the scene's refusal to be quiet or strive for industry-standard perfection.
(Kieran Yates, *Celebrating Channel U's Darren Platt: unsung hero of the UK grime scene,* in *The Guardian,* 15 July 2016)

ACTIVITIES . . .

1. (i) Identify the musical influences that fed into UK Garage. (ii) Which White subculture did UK Garage and Grime influence?

2. How do you think having 35 members with the ability to perform as smaller combinations allowed So Solid Crew to quickly dominate the London scene?

3. What is the significance of Wiley?

4. What is the significance of the Roll Deep crew?

5. According to Source A, what was the significance of *21 Seconds*?

6. According to Source B, how did Grime differ from UK Garage?

EXTENDED WRITING

Write a speech from the first-person perspective of Wiley to younger musicians. Use Sources B, C, and D, and explain (i) how the Grime artists built their popularity, (ii) what obstacles the artists faced, (iii) how the obstacles were similar to or different from Black artists of earlier generations.

Class One: Challenging an Ignorant Historian

Figure 1. David Starkey. (Photo: surreynews). Figure 2. Cartoon caricature of a Chav. (Image: User: J.J.).

Figure 3. Vicky Pollard, *Little Britain* character by Matt Lucas. (Photo: brizzle born and bred).

P.M. 23

Name of Ship ___M.V. "EMPIRE WINDRUSH"___. Port of Arrival ___Tilbury___. Date of Arrival ___21. 6.___ 19 ___48___

Steamship Line ___THE NEW ZEALAND SHIPPING CO. LTD.___. Whence Arrived TRINIDAD, KINGSTON, TAMPICO, HAVANA, BERMUDA.

NAMES AND DESCRIPTIONS OF **BRITISH** PASSENGERS.

(1) Port of Embarkation	(2) Port at which Passengers have been landed	(3) NAMES OF PASSENGERS	(4) CLASS (Whether 1st, 2nd, Tourist or 3rd)	(5) AGES OF PASSENGERS Adults of 12 years and upwards		Children of 1 and 12		Infants		(6) Proposed Address in the United Kingdom	(7) Profession, Occupation, or Calling of Passengers	(8) Country of last Permanent Residence	(9) Country of Intended Future Permanent Residence England / Wales / Scotland / Northern Ireland / Eire / Other parts of the British Empire / Foreign Countries
				Males	Females								
24. TRINIDAD.	Tilbury	DUGDALE Joseph	2A	29						Broxup,Bolton-by-Bowland,Nr.Clitheroe.	Planter.	Trinidad.	
25. "	"	" Stella	"		31					c/o Dir.of Col.Scholars	H.D.	"	
26. "	"	EBHOLE John	"			32				Colonial Office,W.1. St.Catherines Ferree,	Student.	"	
27. "	"	FORBES Mary	"			41				Twickenham,Middlx,	H.D.	British Guiana.	
28. "	"	FRASER Muriel	"			39				Millington,Farmbridge Park,Hants.	Bank Clerk.	England.	
29. "	"	GANDY Adelaide	"			42				41,Hardgate,Aberdeen.	H.D.	Trinidad.	
30. "	"	GRANT Flora	"	59						– do –	"	"	
31. "	"	" Lewis	"	58						75,Martburn Lane,	Merchant.	"	
32. "	"	GALLEY Wilfred	"		25					Launton,Oxon.	Agriculturalist.	Uganda.	
33. "	"	HARRIS Grace	"			45				c/o Lloyds Bank,	H.D.	England.	
34. "	"	HICKSON Audrey	"			39					Nurse	St.Lucia.	
35. "	"	HOOD Hugh	"	39	30					Crescott.	Mariner.	Trinidad.	
36. "	"	KEROY Margaret	"			64				116,Queens Gate,S.W.7.	H.D.		

Figure 4. Passenger List on SS Empire Windrush which arrived on 21 June 1948. The list describes all the people here as British! This is factually correct since all the countries mentioned were parts of the British Empire. Notice also that one passenger was from Uganda!

Figure 5. Arrival at Tilbury Docks, Essex. Figure 6. SS Empire Windrush.

Figure 7. Windrush Square in Brixton, South London, commemorates the SS Empire Windrush. (Photo: Felix-felix~commonswiki).

Class Three: The Calypso Years 1948 – 1962

Figure 8. Lord Kitchener, King of the Calypsonians.   Figure 9. Winifred Atwell, Queen of the Keyboard.

Figure 10. The Trinidad All Steel Percussion Orchestra at *The Festival of Britain*, 1951.

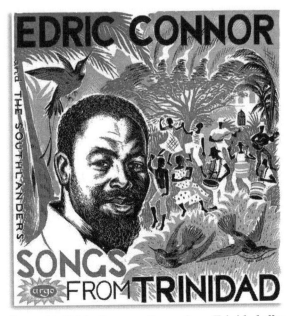

Figure 11. Edric Connor, *Songs from Trinidad* album. Figure 12. *Calypso in Britain 1950 - 1955* compilation.

Figures 13 and 14. Typical headlines highlighting Teddy Boy Violence.

Figure 15. Teddy Boys. (Photo: brizzle born and bred). Figure 16. Fats Domino, pioneer of Rock and Roll.

Figure 17. Chuck Berry, pioneer of Rockabilly.

Figure 18. Cliff Richard and The Shadows. Cliff Richard is second from the right.

Class Five What jobs did Black migrants do?

Figure 19. Charles Gomm, Recruitment Officer for London Transport, with early applicants in Barbados, 1956. Figure 20. This 1962 photograph of Agatha Claudette Hart, Bus Conductor at Stockwell Garage, was used in London Transport's recruitment campaigns.

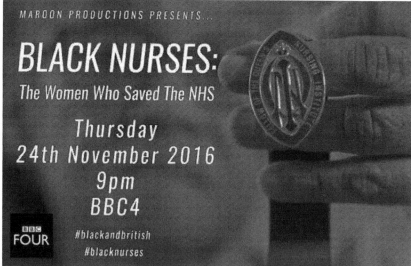

Figure 21. Professor Jacqui Dunkley-Bent with the Duke and Duchess of Cambridge. (Photo: Mark Stewart). Figure 22. Advert for BBC documentary *Black Nurses: The Women Who Saved the NHS.*

Class Six: Anti-Black Violence 1958 – 1959

Figure 23. These types of racist notices were common. Figure 24. Left Wing cartoonist Ken Sprague drew a powerful image of a knife-wielding Teddy Boy killing Kelso Cochrane, urged on by a German Nazi.

Figure 25. Nubian Jak Blue Plaque marking the death of Kelso Cochrane.

78

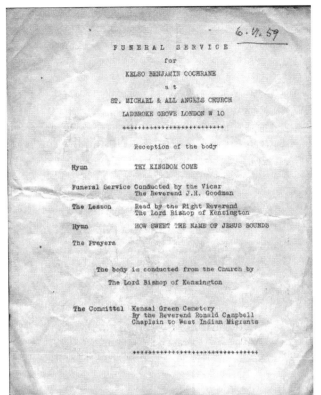

Figure 26. Funeral Programme of Kelso Cochrane. Figure 27. *The Star* reported on the funeral of Kelso Cochrane.

Class Seven: Claudia Jones and the Birth of Carnival

Figure 28. Claudia Jones reading *The West Indian Gazette.* Figure 29. US Commemoration Stamp depicting Claudia Jones.

Figure 30. Limbo Dancing at St Pancras Hall Carnival, 1959.

Figure 31. Guests at St Pancras Hall dancing to the Trinidad All Star Steel Band, 1959.

Figure 32. A young woman parading in Westbourne Grove, Notting Hill Carnival, 2013. (Photo: Romazur).

Class Eight: Origin of Mersey Beat and British Rhythm & Blues 1958 – 1965

Figure 33. The Mersey Beat sound was championed by a fortnightly paper called *Mersey Beat.* Figure 34. The Beatles with Allan and Beryl Williams and Lord Woodbine, Arnhem war memorial, 16 August 1960.

Figure 35. Rolling Stones, 1964. Figure 36. The Rolling Stones' First Album.

Class Nine: The Ska Years 1959 – 1965

Figure 37. Back of an album cover depicting Ska dance moves.

Figure 38. Prince Buster. Figures 39 and 40. Prince Buster, *Madness,* issued in 1963. In England, the Blue Beat label issued the song. This is why Mods called this musical form 'Blue Beat.' Later, a Skinhead / 2 Tone band influenced by Ska, took the name 'Madness'.

Figure 41. *My Boy Lollipop* by Millie, 1964. Figure 42. Ray Charles.

Figure 43. Mods with green overcoats, smart suits with narrow lapels, narrow ties, and scooters.

Figure 44. Old cartoon shows the discrimination against Blacks trying to find accommodation.

Figure 45. KBW graffiti meaning 'Keep Britain White' was a common sight.

Figure 46. 1961 article in the *Bristol Evening Post* revealed the existence of the 'colour bar' against Blacks working on the buses in Bristol. Figure 47. Newspaper article and a letter by a bigoted reader about the Bristol Bus Boycott. Paul Stephenson is in the centre of the picture.

Figure 48. Eight of the Mangrove Nine members are depicted in this paper. The second individual, Radford Howe, is better known as Darcus Howe.

Class Eleven: The Mod Subculture

Figure 49. Prince Buster wearing a narrow lapeled jacket and a thin tie. Figure 50. Mary Quant.

Figure 51. Jimmy James and the Vagabonds. Jimmy James is second from the right. Figure 52. Twisted Wheel club badge. This Mod club started the all-night Northern Soul Scene.

Class Twelve: The Rocksteady Years 1966 – 1969

Figure 53. Desmond Dekker, a pioneer of Rocksteady and role model for the Skinheads. Figure 54. Old photograph of two boys, one of whom is dressed in the Jamaican Rude Boy style.

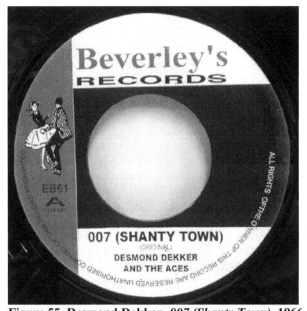 

Figure 55. Desmond Dekker, *007 (Shanty Town),* **1966.** **Figure 56. Derrick Morgan,** *Tougher than Tough.*

Figure 57. Dramatic photograph of Derrick Morgan wearing the Rude Boy staple of a pork pie hat and a jacket with narrow lapels.

Class Thirteen: Enoch Powell and the 'Rivers of Blood' Speech

Figure 58. Enoch Powell delivering his famous rabble-rousing speech, known as the 'Rivers of Blood,' 1968. Figure 59. Enoch Powell is still regarded as a hero by extremists.

Class Fourteen: The Skinhead Subculture

Figure 60. Symarip, *Skinhead Moonstomp,* 1969. This is a classic Reggae album on the Trojan label dedicated to the Skinheads. Figure 61. Some Traditional Skinheads wear the SHARP patch to distinguish themselves from Nazi Skinheads.

Figure 62. The British Movement, a breakaway organisation from the National Front, contained Nazi Skinheads shown sieg-heiling, 1980s.

Class Fifteen: The Reggae Years 1968 – 1978

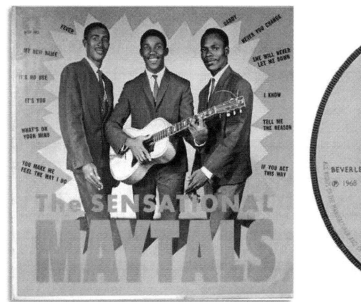

Figure 63. Toots and the Maytals were the pioneers of Reggae.   Figure 64. *Do the Reggay* was the first Reggae recording, 1968.

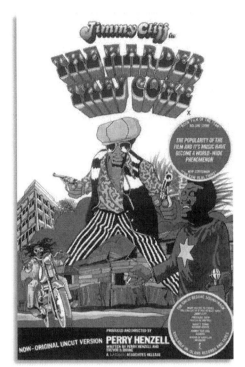
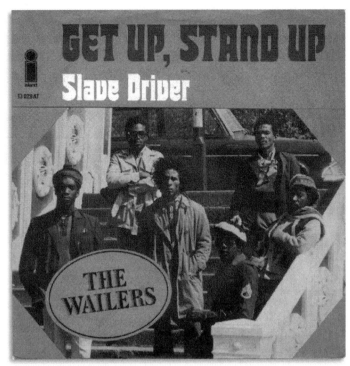

Figure 65. *The Harder They Come,* 1972, film poster. Jimmy Cliff is depicted on the right. **Figure 66.** The Wailers, *Get Up, Stand Up, Slave Driver,* 1974.

Class Sixteen: Notting Hill Carnival 1976

Figure 67. Banner advertising the Notting Hill Carnival 1976.

Figure 68. Police retreating from the violence at Notting Hill, 1 September 1976.

Class Seventeen: The Punk Subculture

Figure 69. Don Letts appeared on the cover of the DIY Punk magazine *Sniffin' Glue,* February 1977. Figure 70. This badge or symbol was commonly worn to promote *Rock Against Racism.*

Figure 71. Sex Pistols in performance, 1977. Figure 72. Splendid Portrait of Poly Styrene, lead singer of X-Ray Spex.

Class Eighteen: The Lovers Rock Years 1975 – 1983

Figure 73. Menelik Shabazz directed the documentary film, *The Story of Lover's Rock,* to remember this era.

Figure 74. Louisa Marks. Figure 75. Janet Kay, *Silly Games,* **1979.**

Class Nineteen: The 2 Tone Years 1978 – 1983

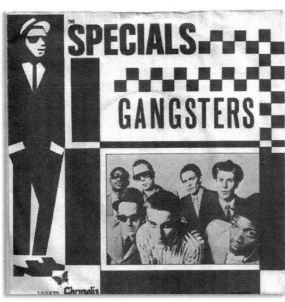

Figure 76. The Specials, *Gangsters,* **1979. Their dress styles encompass Mod, Rude Boy, and Skinhead styles. Jerry Dammers, the founder of 2 Tone, is third from the left. On the left-hand side is the 2 Tone Records logo. Figure 77. Is there a connection between this Peter Tosh album cover and the 2 Tone Records logo?**

Figure 78. Madness logo shows a porkpie hat. Figure 79. Madness took their name from a Prince Buster song entitled 'Madness'. They recorded their version of it in 1979. Figure 80. Bad Manners logo shows a Skinhead with his tongue stuck out. The image is a caricature of the lead singer Buster Bloodvessel.

Class Twenty: The Africanisation of Black Britain

Figure 81. The four main stars of the sitcom *Rising Damp*. Philip Smith, played by Don Warrington, is on the right of the picture. Figure 82. Sir Mo Farah (Somali) at the 2014 European Athletics Championships in Zurich doing his trademark 'Mobot'. (Photo: Erik van Leeuwen, bron: Wikipedia).

Figure 83. Patti Boulaye (Nigerian) album. No Black woman had this type of image or presentation in the UK at the time. Figure 84. Dizzee Rascal (Ghanaian) performing live in 2013. (Photo: Achim Raschka).

Class Twenty-One: 1981: Year of Confrontation

Figure 85. 1981 New Cross Fire blue plaque. Figure 86. Black People's Day of Action to protest the New Cross Fire.

Figure 87. *The Sun* newspaper reporting on the conflicts in Toxteth, Liverpool, 1981. Figure 88. Lord Scarman's Report has been re issued in book form.

Class Twenty-Two: Black Activism and Black History Month UK

Figure 89. Linda Bellos, a leading civil rights figure of the 1980s. Figure 90. Akyaaba Addai Sebbo, founder of Black History Month UK.

Figure 91. *Sunday Express* cartoon typical of the anti Loony Left bigoted nonsense that the papers could get away with in the 1980s.

Figure 92. Black History Month welcome to African American Professor Maulana Karenga by the London Strategic Policy Unit, 1987. Figure 93. Black History Month UK 1987 badge.

Figure 94. Randolph Turpin (right) vs Sugar Ray Robinson (left), 1951.

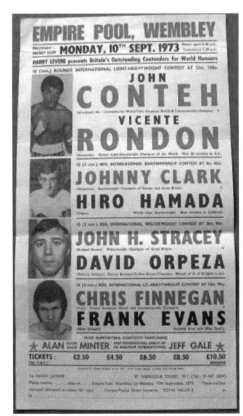

Figure 95. John Conteh on a boxing poster, 1973. Figure 96. John Conteh on the front cover of *The Sunday Times Magazine*.

Figure 97. Frank Bruno. Figure 98. Nigel Benn vs Chris Eubank, 1993 poster.

Class Twenty-Four: Entering the Mainstream – Athletics

Figure 99. Daley Thompson signed memorabilia advertising Adidas, 1984. Figure 100. London street sign named after Daley Thompson. There is also a mention of Tessa Sanderson Place, named after another great Olympian.

Figure 101. 1996 Envelope with a design featuring Tessa Sanderson.

Figure 102. McDonald Bailey sprinting in 1948.

Figure 103. Christine Ohuruogu at the Beijing Olympics, 2008.

99

Figure 104. Clyde Best card. Back in the day, football fans used to collect these cards. Figure 105. The real Three Degrees, an African American Soul trio, photographed with Cyrille Regis, Laurie Cunningham, and Brendon Batson, 3 brilliant footballers nicknamed 'The Three Degrees', 1979.

Figure 106. Viv Anderson card. Figure 107. 1998 Commemorative English Football Team Coin depicting Paul Ince.

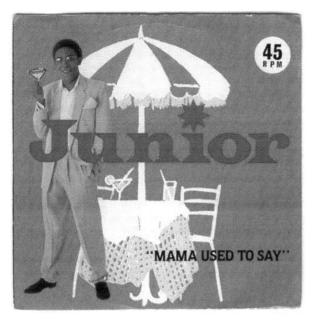

Figure 108. Junior, *Mama Used to Say*. Figure 109. Sade, *Smooth Operator*.

Figure 110. Loose Ends, *Hangin' on a String*. Figure 111. Soul II Soul, *Back To Life (However Do You Want Me)*. Their cool dreadlocked appearance contrasted with suit and tie image of earlier 1980s British Soul artists.

Figure 112. M Beat featuring General Levy, *Incredible*.   Figure 113. Shy FX and UK Apachi, *Original Nuttah*.

Figure 114. Congo Natty, *Junglist*.

Figure 115. Andrew Salkey. Figure 116. Andrew Salkey, *A Quality of Violence*, 1959.

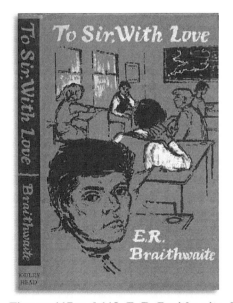

Figures 117 and 118. E. R. Braithwaite, *To Sir, With Love*, 1959. This book was turned into a film starring the great Sidney Poitier and the Scottish Beat musician, Lulu.

Figure 119. Andrea Levy, *Small Island,* **2004. Figure 120. BBC advert for the televised drama series based on the book,** *Small Island.*

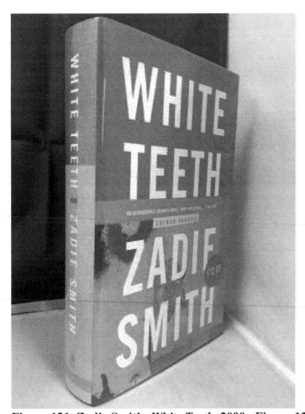
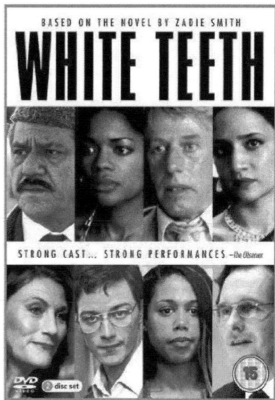

Figure 121. Zadie Smith, *White Teeth,* **2000. Figure 122. This was televised as a Channel 4 drama series.**

Figure 123. *Love Thy Neighbour* advertising poster. Rudolph Walker is the second from the right. Figure 124. *Desmond's* advertising. Carmen Munroe and Norman Beaton are fifth and sixth from the right.

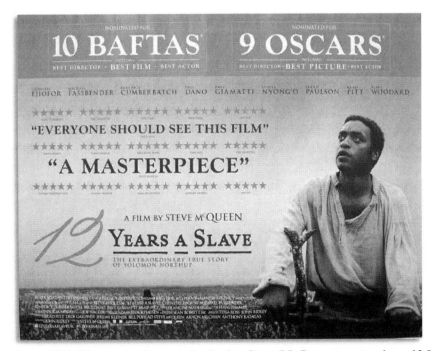

Figure 125. Film poster for award winning Steve McQueen masterpiece, *12 Years a Slave*. Chiwetel Ejiofor was the lead in the film. Figure 126. Sophie Okonedo at the Tony Awards, 2014.

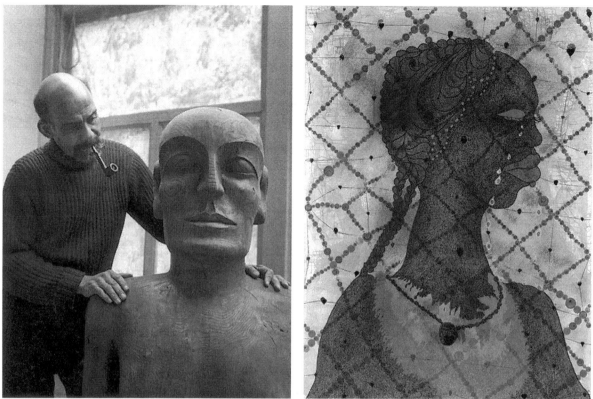

Figure 127. Ronald Moody with his sculpture *Johaanan* carved in 1936. Figure 128. Christopher Ofili, *No Woman No Cry*, 1998, dedicated to Lady Doreen Lawrence on the murder of her son. (Photo: Wikipedia).

Figure 129. Yinka Shonibare, *Nelson's Ship in a Bottle*. (Photo: Wikipedia).

106

Figure 130. *A Man's Story* film poster on the life and career of the Savile Row tailor Ozwald Boateng.

Figures 131 and 132. Naomi Campbell on the front cover of an all-Black edition of *Vogue Italia.* She is also depicted on an Austrian stamp.

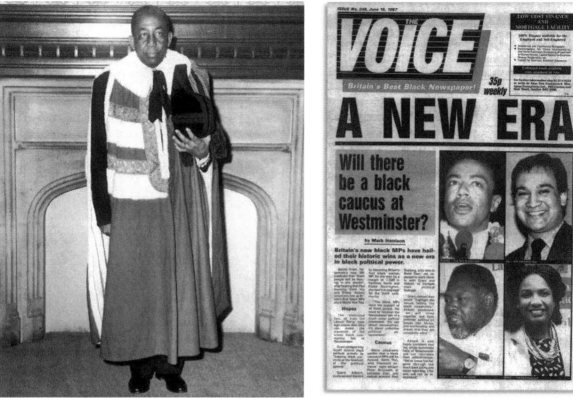

Figure 133. Sir Learie Constantine joins the House of Lords as Baron Constantine of Maraval and Nelson, 1969. Figure 134. *The Voice* newspaper carried a front page on the election of Black MPs in 1987: Paul Boateng, Keith Vaz, Bernie Grant and Diane Abbott.

Figure 135. Debate at the House of Lords, 2010. Lord Morris of Handsworth is front left. Lady Scotland of Asthal is seated behind. (Photo: parliamentary copyright).

Figure 136. Lady Valerie Amos of Brondesbury.   Figure 137. The Archbishop of York, Dr John Sentamu.

Class Thirty-Two: The Garage and Grime Years 2000 – 2016

Figure 138. Advert for the So Solid Crew performing at the MOBO Awards, 2013.

Figure 139. Wiley, *The Ascent* album cover.   Figure 140. The Roll Deep Crew.

Figure 141. Tinchy Stryder.

110

History is a powerful subject for changing perceptions and challenging stereotypes. Black History is particularly urgent since far right extremism is increasingly back on the march across Europe. We hope that schoolteachers and parents grasp the importance of the content presented here and lobby their schools to use it.

Academies, Free Schools, Independent Schools, and most State Boarding Schools do not have to follow the National Curriculum. These institutions have academic freedom. They can shape courses in response to the academic needs and wants of their pupils, parents, and other stakeholders. Therefore, they should have no academic reasons for overlooking the content presented here.

With the State Schools, however, the situation is different. They must adhere to the National Curriculum. What does this document say about Black British History? Is there space for it on the National Curriculum? If so, where?

The Department of Education, following the lead of Mr Michael Gove, published *History programmes of study: key stage 3, National curriculum in England* in September 2013. The first part of the document set out the 'Purpose of study.' The document states:

A high-quality history education will help pupils gain a coherent knowledge and understanding of Britain's past and that of the wider world. It should inspire pupils' curiosity to know more about the past. Teaching should equip pupils to ask perceptive questions, think critically, weigh evidence, sift arguments, and develop perspective and judgement. History helps pupils to understand the complexity of people's lives, the process of change, the diversity of societies and relationships between different groups, as well as their own identity and the challenges of their time.

Our book, *Black British History: Black Influences on British Culture (1948 to 2016)*, addresses these ambitions in several ways.

Britain's past is historically linked to the wider world of Africa, North America, South America, and the Caribbean. Our content demonstrates this connection. We have made the African, American, and Caribbean subjects of the British Empire, and their migration to Britain, the focus of our study.

We inspire pupil's curiosity to learn more by including topics more diverse than just Political and Social History. We have included Music, Fashion, Sport, Art, Carnival, Literature, and Drama.

We direct pupils to ask and answer controversial historical and social questions about culture and identity. Our activities require pupils to exercise the historical skills of critical thinking, judging evidence, and deciding between conflicting arguments. This helps pupils to develop their own perspectives on an important chapter of British heritage.

Finally, our book offers content that is historically complex. It focuses on change, diversity, relationships between groups, the challenges this poses for groups, and shifting notions of identity. Modern Black Britain is a constantly evolving identity. It was formed out of a melting pot of peoples migrating from different continents with different religious and social class backgrounds. The cultures that emerged from these groups impacted on the Host Communities and other Black Britons in varied and interesting ways. We highlight the challenges and the triumphs of these interactions.

The second part of the National Curriculum document identifies six sets of 'Aims.' Our content directly addresses four of them (i.e. the first, fourth, fifth and sixth) that we have reproduced here. The document states:

The national curriculum for history aims to ensure that all pupils:
- *know and understand the history of these islands as a coherent, chronological narrative, from the earliest times to the present day: how people's lives have shaped this nation and how Britain has influenced and been influenced by the wider world*
- *understand historical concepts such as continuity and change, cause and consequence, similarity, difference and significance, and use them to make connections, draw contrasts, analyse trends, frame historically-valid questions and create their own structured accounts, including written narratives and analyses*
- *understand the methods of historical enquiry, including how evidence is used rigorously to make historical claims, and discern how and why contrasting arguments and interpretations of the past have been constructed*
- *gain historical perspective by placing their growing knowledge into different contexts, understanding the connections between local, regional, national and international history; between cultural, economic, military, political, religious and social history; and between short- and long-term timescales.*

Our book reveals that Britain in the present day cannot be understood without the Black British historical component. Almost all British youth subcultures since the Teddy Boys show obvious Black cultural influences. Moreover, British popular music, a major cultural export, has continued to borrow from Black influences. It is impossible to analyse the lives of British teenagers over the last sixty years without reference to Black Migrant, African American and Black British cultures.

Black Britain has shown some continuity since 1948 but has changed through the absorption of newer movements of Black people bringing new cultural influences. Modern Black British culture was originally Trinidadian, and then Jamaican influenced. Migrants brought these cultures here. By the 1970s, a new Black British culture emerged amongst Blacks born in Britain. Added to this, new Black Migrants brought African cultures to Britain: Nigerian, Ghanaian, and Somali.

Our activities require pupils to exercise all the historical skills specified by the National Curriculum document especially cause and consequence, similarity and difference, and significance. Moreover, the pupils are encouraged to produce their own accounts using a variety of written forms: diary entry, first person account, newspaper article, business pitch, speech, dialogue, debate, persuasive writing, and structured essay.

We require the pupils to use and interrogate a variety of evidence: documents, interviews, televised accounts, blue plaques, photographs, cartoons, badges, memorabilia, and road signs. Moreover, pupils are shown how to address contrasting interpretations and bias.

Finally, our content requires the pupils to focus on a seventy-year period dealing primarily with the area of culture. The time covered is between a short and a long-term time scale.

The third part of the National Curriculum document briefly discusses 'Attainment targets.' The fourth part details 'Subject content Key stage 3.' An excerpt from this section states:

Pupils should be taught about: ...
challenges for Britain, Europe and the wider world 1901 to the present day
In addition to studying the Holocaust, this could include:

> ***Examples (non-statutory)***
> - *women's suffrage*
> - *The First World War and the Peace Settlement*
> - *the inter-war years: the Great Depression and the rise of dictators*
> - *the Second World War and the wartime leadership of Winston Churchill*
> - *the creation of the Welfare State*
> - *Indian independence and end of Empire*
> - *social, cultural and technological change in post-war British society*
> - *Britain's place in the world since 1945*

One suggested area of content for 'challenges for Britain, Europe and the wider world 1901 to the present day' is 'social, cultural and technological change in post-war British society.' Our content, ***Black British History: Black Influences on British Culture (1948 to 2016)*** meets these criteria exactly.

The Historical Association helped to write the history portion of the draft document for The Department of Education in February 2013. The paper was called ***The National Curriculum in England: Framework document for consultation.*** An excerpt from the section on 'The twentieth century' instructs that pupils should be taught, among other things:

- *the Windrush generation, wider new Commonwealth immigration, and the arrival of East African Asians*

At first sight, this draft suggestion of February 2013 appears to be very different to the actual wording of the finalised document published in September 2013. The finalised document says: 'social, cultural and technological change in post-war British society.' Is this the same thing worded differently?

After the finalised document was published, the Historical Association objected to it. They accused the Department of Education of ignoring their advice by radically rewriting the February 2013 draft. In addition, the Historical Association uploaded their objections on to their website in a document entitled: ***Reform of the National Curriculum in England: Consultation Response Form.*** Of the many things the Historical Association found objectionable in the finalised document, was the treatment of Black British History. To quote them directly:

[T]he first time Black history in Britain is really treated in the content is through Windrush. As this occurs in the chronological order at Key Stage 3, this seriously limits what primary schools are able to do. It also provides students with a skewed perception. In fact, immigration itself is poorly dealt with, being limited to the early settlers, Windrush and East African Asians.

This suggests that the Historical Association think that the finalised document DOES accept Windrush as part of Key Stage 3 History. But where is that explicitly stated in the finalised document?

We conclude that the phrase 'social, cultural and technological change in post-war British society' is a direct reference to Windrush (also Commonwealth immigration and East African Asians). It seems that the Department of Education chose to use language in the finalised document that was deceptively vague. Whichever be the case, this shows there are no academic reasons for State Schools to overlook the content presented here.

All willing schools can use this content: Academies, Free Schools, Independent Schools, State Boarding Schools, and State Schools.

Robin Walker 'The Black History Man' was born in London but has also lived in Jamaica. He attended the London School of Economics and Political Science where he read Economics. In 1991 and 1992, he studied African World Studies with the brilliant Dr Femi Biko and later with Mr Kenny Bakie. Between 1993 and 1994, he trained as a secondary school teacher at Edge Hill College (linked to the University of Lancaster). In 2006, he wrote the seminal *When We Ruled.* It is the most advanced synthesis on Ancient and Mediaeval African history ever written by a single author. It established his reputation as the leading Black History educational service provider. Between 2013 and 2015, he wrote *When We Ruled: Second Edition, When We Ruled Study Guide and Reading Plan, Blacks and Science Volumes I, II and III, Blacks and Religion Volumes I and II, The Rise and Fall of Black Wall Street and the Seven Key Empowerment Lessons, The Black Musical Tradition and Early Black Literature* and *19 Lessons in Black History.* He also wrote two books in collaboration with others: *Everyday Life in an Early West African Empire* and *African Mathematics: History, Study Guide and Classroom Lessons.*

To book Robin as a workshop leader, lecturer or staff trainer, email historicalwalker@yahoo.com

Vanika Marshall was born in London of Jamaican parents. She grew up in Streatham and Croydon and educated in the Croydon and Selsdon areas. At the tender age of 12, Vanika began reading *The Destruction of Black Civilization* by Chancellor Williams, for the first time. This keen interest in Black History has remained strong. Vanika has studied with and completed African History courses with Black History Studies, Robin Walker, and Onyeka Nubia. Fascinated by the African links to this country, Vanika often attends Tony Warner's Black History Walks events. Vanika is currently a volunteer for the 100 Black Men of London organisation and was a mentor on their Community Mentoring Programme for 3 consecutive years. She is also a volunteer teacher at a Saturday School in Croydon and enjoys helping out at various events within the community. Vanika is proud to be a part of this work which highlights the Black influences in British culture. She believes the information presented here will bring awareness to those learning about it for the first time. It also serves as a reminder to others, regarding the history of this country that this information must continue to be passed on.

To book Vanika as a lecturer, email V33Marsh@gmail.com

Anthony Vaughan was born in England of Jamaican parents. He received a BA Honours Degree from East London University. He is particularly proud of a project he completed with the great C. L. R. James called *Cultural Conversations with C. L. R. James.* This original research is now with the Black Cultural Archives in Brixton, South London. He also has a Certificate in Education F.E. Communications and Special Needs. He has lectured at Croydon College.

To book Anthony as a lecturer, email avaughan90@gmail.com

Paula Perry is known as the 'Cycle Breaking Coach'. She has over 14 years of experience as a Project Manager managing multi-million-pound budgets across London where she gained extensive experience in economic regeneration. During this time, she became concerned that projects within communities were only providing surface level support to members (i.e. young people, the unemployed and small businesses) and not addressing the deep-rooted issues they faced. Consequently, she started You4Us which is dedicated to empowering families and creating a domino effect that breaks the negative cycle of generational poverty in areas such as Finance, Education, Parenting, and Spirituality. Before setting up her company You4Us Paula volunteered at her local youth club for several years (a place she had also attended) and arranged workshops with the aim of increasing life aspirations, confidence, and self-belief where the environment did not allow for these characteristics to be normal. Her aim was for young people to believe that no matter what their circumstances were, they could achieve their hearts desires by adopting the right mindset. Through her ability to genuinely relate to their issues, Paula has used her personal experiences as a young person as the blueprint for achieving her destiny and has proved successful in impacting adults and young people in the UK and Internationally.

To book Paula as a lecturer, email paulaperry@you4us.com

Also available.

INDEX

Printed in Poland
by Amazon Fulfillment
Poland Sp. z o.o., Wrocław